No, gracefully

No, gracefully

Learning to Say No with Confidence:
Taking Charge of Your Life Begins Here.

Reclaim your autonomy by putting
an end to people pleasing.

Nubia C. Santos, Ph.D., L.M.H.C., C.S.T.

© 2017 **Nubia C. Santos, Ph.D., L.M.H.C., C.S.T.**
All rights reserved.

ISBN-13: **9781542312455**
ISBN-10: **1542312450**
Library of Congress Control Number: **2017900199**
CreateSpace Independent Publishing Platform
North Charleston, South Carolina

Table of Contents

Disclaimer

The content of this book is intended to educate readers and to provide insight and tools that may be useful in their personal and interpersonal development. However, the content of this book is *not* intended to replace individualized help from a professional.

The case studies presented in this book were inspired by real-life cases I encountered in my psychotherapy practice, and through acquaintances of mine. Therefore, in order to protect the anonymity of my patients, these cases represent a compilation of behavioral patterns identified from real situations, and they do not specifically describe any specific one case.

Lastly, for better flow, "he" and "she" will be used interchangeably throughout the book.

MY OBSERVATIONS AS A THERAPIST

As a therapist, I have observed the violation of self-boundaries to be a common theme among people from all walks of life. People often agree to take on more than they can realistically handle by overcommitting;accepting requests they do not want to or cannot do. By saying "yes," favors become burdens, which creates problems, disrupts relationships, and causes bottled-up resentment. Failing to set healthy interpersonal boundaries interferes with a person's life flow and creates unnecessary life obstacles.

Often people seek my services to treat their symptoms of depression and anxiety, low self-esteem, sexual and relational problems, and to assist them with their overall life goals. These include become more productive, increase their motivation, develop and maintaining new healthier habits, improve communication within their romantic relationships, and increase the quality of their sex life, to name a few.

Frequently, when assessing these individuals' cases, it becomes evident that the main obstacle in the way of their personal growth, and overall mental health is their habitual violation of self-boundaries. These individuals have been practicing pleasing others, and over time, find themselves puzzled and unaware of how they have arrived at their current mental state.

These individuals' motivations and actions tend to be guided by the priorities of other people, which typically tend to have a negative impact in the overall well-being of a person, across all of his or her life arenas. For example, people who tend to violate their own needs for the needs of others are often unhappy, and they share that trait with others who tend to have problems saying "no." These folks also tend to blame other people for their own life dissatisfactions.

Typically, these individuals' primary complaints are about others or about the situation—in other words, they externalize the blame onto a source outside of their own perceived control, which causes these individuals to experience resentfulness, irritability, and anger. As a result, these clients suffer from a state of low self-esteem. As we dig deeper, the observed patterns of symptoms these clients share are frequently associated with the habitual self-violation of boundaries. Specifically, a tendency to say "yes" when the person means "no." Violating your own personal boundaries with the needs of others is not sustainable. Consistently saying "yes," when you mean "no," can lead to disruption of your own life, your relationships, and eventually self-exhaustion.

In my practice, symptoms of violation of self-boundaries have been presented in a number of ways, including:

- "Agreeing" with others when you do not actually agree (with what is being said or done).
- The inability to break ties with those whom you no longer wish to have a relationship with.
- A fear of upsetting others by declining their requests for favors.
- Being unable to make yourself unavailable to others, regardless of how this impacts your own life.
- Attempting to avoid future feelings of guilt by making commitments that you know you will later regret.
- Experiencing overwhelming feelings of guilt when unable to stick to these commitments.
- Holding other people responsible for your own happiness.
- Feeling stuck in a relationship.

When you say "yes" when you really mean "no," you are "pleasing" in an attempt to avoid the reaction or disapproval of another person. You are attempting to control something which is not within your control; another person.

I have explored the existing research literature and investigated a number of cases that I have treated to increase my understanding of the concept of pleasing. Over time, it has become evident to me that pleasing is a habit that evolves with consistent practice and eventually becomes a habit that is far from adaptive to a person's life. As a habit, the process of thinking and acting in a pleasing manner is often automatic; it has become second nature to the pleaser.

Again, being a "skilled" pleaser does not promote healthy adjustment of a person in his environment. Being a pleaser contributes to poor interpersonal relationships across one or more settings of life. Being a pleaser implicates how we relate to ourselves and other people. For example, pleasing impairs your ability to develop and maintain a healthy self-connection, which impairs your ability to develop and maintain healthy connections with others. Generally, being a pleaser appears to be negatively correlated to one's degree of self-worth.

My investigations and observations relating to this topic have revealed the need to please others as being associated with development. The behavior is often traced back to a person's earlier experiences, and sometimes to more recent stages of life. For example, as the result of a significant relationship.

I have also noticed the habit of pleasing to sometimes have generational roots, as it gets passed down from older generations. In other words, there is an environmental influence on a person's way of thinking and behaving with themselves and others.

Over time, I have become confident that the problems of many who come to seek my services are rooted in their habitual violation of self-boundaries, a maladaptive coping survival mechanism learned and developed from prior experiences and the ongoing practice of these behaviors. Everyone has heard the tried and true phrase, "practice makes perfect." Well, the same is just as true when it comes to practicing bad habits.

It is important to recognize that in order to establish healthy boundaries with other people, you need to first develop healthy boundaries with yourself. You are, after all, the one who draws the line between you and another, and you are the one who informs others about your limits.

First, you must decide what your limits are so you can better communicate them to others. To do this, you must become aware of what your priorities are when it comes to tasks, relationships with others, and goals. Then, when you are asked for a favor, you can ask yourself how that action might bring you closer to your goals, or how that action might deter you from your goals. Continually ask yourself if agreeing to do the favor is something you really want to do, or even if you have the ability and skills to do it.

For example, let's say you have decided to take yoga classes after work. For the past two weeks, however, you have been providing emotional support to a friend who is experiencing relationship problems with her partner. Every time you attempt to drive to your yoga class you find yourself stuck in the car talking to your friend. On top of that, you have also been texting back and forth with this friend during work hours. She calls you the minute you are out of work, and as a result of her own life crises, you once again miss your yoga class.

This pattern has left you with feelings of frustration every night, and you do not have anyone to vent your own frustrations to. In other words, you continue to say "yes" when you mean "no," in this case your behavior is not aligning with your goal (yoga classes after work). It is understandable that your friend needs you, but it is also reasonable for you to not provide her with this level of attention if it consistently interferes with your own happiness.

It is important to understand that helping other people does not require you to give ALL of you, so that there is nothing left for yourself and other people in your life. It is also important to consider that not all relationships and situations deserve the same level of priority, and no one necessarily needs to suffer at the cost of the other. Having effective boundary skills involves self-respect and respect toward other people.

WHAT IS THE PURPOSE OF THIS BOOK?

- To help you develop awareness of the role you play in violating your own boundaries.
- To help you understand how your violation of self-boundaries is implicated in other aspects of your life, including your relationships with others.
- To help you learn to develop and implement healthy boundaries, and regain your autonomy and independence.
- To help you become self-empowered.

WHAT TO EXPECT TO FIND IN THIS BOOK

This book will provide helpful tools to assist you increase your interpersonal effectiveness, through improving your ability to communicate your needs and wants effectively by improving your ability to say "no," and by consequently providing you with an increased ability to form and foster positive relationships.

In addition, the chapters include educational content necessary for the process of developing your self-awareness. The educational content will not only help you to better understand yourself and allow you to improve your self-awareness, but it will also contribute to promoting changes in the way you perceive yourself and others, which can lead to improved interpersonal skills.

The material is intended to educate the reader on how the perception of an individual is developed and how it can be changed for the better. This book should also help you to identify the source of your own boundary issues, and how it affects you and your relationships. Finally, the book will help you to address other symptoms that may result from consistently violating your self-boundaries. These may include, fears, anxieties, and feelings of associated guilt, as well as irrational thoughts, and negative irrational beliefs you may hold of yourself. Hopefully, the reading will also assist you in identifying the common theme of your relational patterns *(how you love)* across the relationships you have been able to cultivate and retain; or help you understand more about the relationships you have lost.

HOW THE BOOK IS STRUCTURED

The book is divided into two parts. The first part is geared to educate you about the topic, and to help you identify how the topic uniquely connects with you. Although the first part of the book mostly consists of information, which might read slightly dense at times, it also includes reflection exercises that will keep the reader active in the process. The second part, includes information that is more practical in nature, along with additional reflection exercises. In-text numbers corresponding to the reference list are used instead of in-text citations. Case examples are included throughout the book. The case examples may not be 100% accurate representations of your specific life situation. However, you are encouraged to maintain an open-minded approach and take away the aspects of these cases as a whole. The Appendix section includes some tips to help you begin the process of becoming more self-focused. In this section I provide strategies to help you to make time to read this book and other books similar to this one, read this book more effectively, and reflect.

MY HOPES AND GOALS FOR THE READER

It is my hope that the framework of the next chapters will provide you with useful information that can help you attain healthier relational assertiveness, and improve your overall relationship capacity. This includes breaking patterns of maladaptive internal and external habits of pleasing others, controlling your impulses to please, and reframing your perspective from being the subjective pleaser to an objective creator of your reality. Even a small degree of change that can improve how you relate with others will make you feel better about yourself, increase your self-worth, help you to feel more respected by others, and decrease the anxiety that results from pleasing others as a way to feel accepted.

Simply put, it is my hope that this book will contribute to an increase in your overall well-being. I strongly encourage you to take ten to fifteen minutes from your day to do the reflections included in each of the chapters.

Healthy Boundaries and Beyond

Saying "no" is a key ingredient in healthy interpersonal boundaries—a crucial component in the well-being of a person and the success of all types of relationships. This is because having healthy interpersonal boundaries is an indicator of a healthy balance between individual autonomy and being together with other people. Establishing healthy interpersonal boundaries requires people to clearly express their individual wants and needs; often, this is accomplished by saying "no." Healthy boundaries begin with oneself;it is necessary to know what we want as individuals, including our own personal limits, before we say "yes" or "no" to another person or situation.

Practicing healthy boundaries is necessary for the optimal health of the whole person and his or her relationships. Individuals who practice maintaining healthy boundaries, do not allow themselves to become depleted as a result of consistently tending to the needs of other people. Having healthy boundaries enhances your social competence. Individuals who possess healthy interpersonal boundaries know what they want and need, and they communicate these wants and needs clearly to other people. Others are therefore not left to guess the needs of the individual, which would almost inevitably leads to failure to give the person what they truly need or want.

Boundaries are an important element for enhancing and preserving a person and his or her relationships. It is hard to imagine life without this skill. Yet, the majority of us are likely to consistently violate our own boundaries instead. The good news is that, one can learn to implement healthy boundaries, and this book offers useful knowledge and tools that can help increase your ability to develop and maintain a healthier relationship with yourself, as well as healthier relationships with others.

As a skill, setting your own interpersonal boundaries can be improved through learning and practice, which will likely require stepping out of yourcomfort zone. This is because, for many, even the thought of learning and practicing a new skill in the context of relationships causes discomfort. Nevertheless, the benefits of establishing boundaries will far outweigh any initial feelings of discomfort, as it is can be the key to a person's overall health and the health of their relationships with others.

Frequently, one of the reasons why we do not assert our limits is that we are afraid of the potential disapproval of others. We feel unsettled by the fact that we really have no way of knowing what the other person would really think about us if we were to decline them. The reality is that pleasing is actually a form of control. We are subconsciously attempting to control the other person's reaction, or perception of us, by going out of our way to please them. Maybe you accept a new task because you want your boss to view you as a go-getter even though you already have too much on your plate. Or perhaps you want to be perceived as easy-going and fun by your friends, so you always agree to go out on the weekend, even though you would rather stay in.

Another reason we fail to assert limits can be because we want to be appreciated by other people. We may come to expect certain signs of appreciation or gratitude as a reward for our willingness to go out of our way for others. The problem here is that we almost always find ourselves disappointed in these cases. For example, the other person may not be aware that you perceived their request as a burden, but decided to do it anyway. In such a case, they may not think a grand gesture of gratitude is necessary or expected. In fact, most likely, they would prefer that you decline their request if they knew how much you resented doing it or that you expected anything in return. In Chapter 2, we will discuss more about reasons why people please.

In contrast, asserting limits in front of others establishes that you are honest and predictable in the way you feel about a person or a situation, and that other people do not have to worry about what you are thinking, because you are good at communicating it yourself. In other words, communicating your needs and wants clearly contributes to positive dynamics in relationships that are free of ambiguity.

So, despite what our intuition may tell us, the practice of consistently establishing boundaries, often makes a good impression on others. Let us dive into this concept a little deeper, by looking at the case of Andrew.

Andrew

Andrew adores helping people. He is a registered volunteer for at least three different organizations that promote the wellbeing of children from the dependency system and the wellbeing of underprivileged families of young single mothers. Andrew wishes he had more time to spend helping these organizations, but between his demanding career; time for his own self-care (which includes his daily exercise routine); cooking his own meals; his Saturday-morning basketball games with his buddies; time for sleeping; his lovely girlfriend, Sophie; his friends and family; and Gus, his energetic and very large Labrador puppy, Andrew is doing the best that he can.

Andrew is well-liked by many, including his family, his coworkers, his girlfriend, and Gus—of course. Those who know Andrew think of him as a good friend who truly cares about the wellbeing of others and who is always willing to help. However, his friends will also assure you that while Andrew is always *willing* to help, he does not always help. Andrew is very honest, and when he is unable to assist someone, or if he is unhappy about someone's specific behavior, he will be sure to communicate his thoughts with respect and clarity. This is one of Andrew's traits that those closest to him seem to really appreciate him for.

Andrew's friends describe him as warm and assertive, in that he cares for the feelings of others, while at the same time he is able to communicate his own needs and wants clearly. Andrew's honesty, warmth, and regard for those around him and for people in general, coupled with his self-regard, are what makes relating with him a stable and predictable experience. This predictability is what provides stability and safety for those around him. For instance, Andrew's ability to say "no" effectively creates opportunities for others to trust him and relax around him, because they do not feel the need to "figure him out." Instead, the people around Andrew have established expectations of stability in the dynamic of their relationship with him.

Andrew typically does not allow himself to be imposed upon by others to only become resentful by the imposition—instead, he practices doing things for others out of his own desire to do these things—and as a rule, he will generally tell you how he feels. In other words, it is typical for Andrew to express his thoughts clearly instead of leaving it up to others to figure out what he wants and needs.

Instead, unlike Andrew, many of us are unable to communicate our wants and needs. Many of us are simply unable to say "no." We frequently commit ourselves to doing favors for other people when we are unable or unwilling to do these acts. Then, afterward, we only become bitter toward the other person for making the request and for the negative impact that accepting the request had on us. Does this sound familiar?

Just as when we wish to say "no" but instead say "yes," it is a subconscious decision, and the same may be true for Andrew when he says "no." Practicing healthy boundaries with himself and others has become second nature to him. In other words, it has formed into a habit, which is practiced outside of his awareness. So, unless Andrew's ability to form boundaries was pointed out to him, it's possible he would never become aware of the fact that he has this skill.

Andrew's overall perception of his friends and other relationships tends to be more positive, because Andrew feels autonomous in his relationships with others. He does not put himself in situations where he is blaming others for feeling overwhelmed and abused. Andrew knows that he is in charge of deciding what works, or what doesn't work for him. When Andrew says yes to someone or something, it most frequently comes from a place of want instead of from subconscious attempts to control the reactions of others, or to be appreciated for his good deeds. Additionally, his ability to determine his own needs and wants and to communicate these clearly makes him feel responsible for his own choices instead of holding others responsible for his actions. So, when Andrew says "yes" it means yes, regardless of whether others appreciate him for it or not.

Like Andrew, some of us are better than others at saying "no." Even those who are quite good at saying "no" can fail to set limits at times. In some situations, our ability to establish healthy limits with others is not consistent across all settings of our lives. For example, you may be good at setting limits at work while you struggle to set limits with your family at home. In any case, the outcome of these interactions with others, depends on one's ability to first observe their own boundaries which they have set for themselves.

Interpersonal boundaries refer to a person's ability to set healthy limits with others, or the ability to say "no" effectively, which means communicating your intentions clearly and respectfully with others. This ability comes from a healthy sense of self—from being able to be assertive.

Intrapersonal boundaries, in contrast, refers to limits you set with yourself in relation to your self-worth and self-respect. In other words, you set the line of your worth so others know where to meet you at. So, saying "no" to yourself—and setting your own intrapersonal boundaries—is the first thing you must do before you attempt to establish interpersonal boundaries (with other people). For instance, when someone else requests something from you, you must first ask yourself if this is something you want to do or can do. If the answer to yourself is "no," then this is the answer you should also give, politely and assertively, to the other person.

It is important to keep in mind the various ways in which we may be saying yes to others, even without saying the word "yes". For example, sometimes when you do not say anything, your silence can mean that you are in agreement. Consider the case of Ana.

Josie invited Ana to dinner to meet Gabi, her best friend from childhood who was visiting from out of town. As a nice gesture to her visiting friend, Josie decided that Ana and she should pick up the tab for her friend, and on the spot, Josie announced this imposition on Ana. Ana did not like being put in an awkward situation, but she could not bring herself to say "no." Quietly, Ana swallowed her frustration and paid for half of Josie's friend's dinner tab. Eventually, this made Ana feel resentful toward herself for not saying "no" to Josie's imposition, and resentful toward Josie for imposing it in the first place.

By conforming quietly with Josie's imposition, Ana communicated her agreement, which is the same as saying "yes." Ana also came to realize that this was not the first time Josie had imposed on her and she had silently accepted. Regardless of what Josie's intentions were, this situation illustrates the concept that we are responsible for our own boundaries with others, and if we do not communicate them, it opens the door for others do what they need/or want to do for themselves.

Here are some of the many ways of unintentionally saying "yes" to others:

- Not saying anything
- Continuing to act against your will
- Not expressing your opinion; instead, taking the passive role in a situation or interaction, which communicates to others that you agree with them
- Not attempting to stop others from behaving in ways that are negatively impacting you
- Staying in situations that do not work for you

- Constantly complaining to irrelevant people, instead of the person you have attributed your feelings to
- Continuing to do for others what others can do for themselves
- Not taking charge of your own life
- Not make the necessary changes/adjustments needed to change what isn't working for you

As previously discussed in the beginning of this chapter, when you do not deny a request because you cannot bring yourself to say "no," you are in fact attempting to control the other person's reaction toward you. As we have seen, however, clear communication of boundaries often leads others to view you in a more positive light than simply agreeing to everything, because it is more honest.

Another thing to consider is that, after a while, failing to assert your limits with others becomes taxing on you and your life. You begin to complain about how your boss does not respect your personal life and family; your partner is unfair and unwilling to help; your kids only call you for money; your friends only call you when they do not have anyone else to go out with; and you start feeling that there are no good people left in the world. Although you blame and resent others for not recognizing your efforts of pleasing them, most of the resentment is toward yourself. That is because you have become disappointed in your own lack of assertiveness, self-advocacy, and failure to protect yourself from being unappreciated or flat-out abused.

It is fair to say that, when you leave it to others to decide what you need and want, you will most likely not get what you want and need because each person's perception of an experience is unique to that individual, and as such, others simply do not know what is best for you. Also, your needs may not be a priority for the other person, or they might not know what your limits consist of. Saying "yes" when you mean "no," does not effectively communicate to others your true intent and desire. If this is your usual pattern, you have trained those around you to expect your yes*es*. This causes you to develop unrealistic expectations of others, and again more than likely you will be disappointed every time.

We are all responsible for asserting and sustaining our own individuality within the context of our relationships, and this is established independently from others. If we each accept this responsibility, then the context of relationships provides the opportunity for individuals to exchange altruistic intentions and gestures; grow individually and relationally; and build together an environment that is safe for both to communicate their own needs and wants, to regard and be regarded, and to appropriately care for one another.

My purpose is not to advocate against saying yes to others. Instead, my attempt here is to help you to identify your very own healthy levels of yes*es* and no*s*. Humans have an innate need to connect with others, which includes the need to have opportunities to care for one another, to care for other living things such as other people, pets, and plants, and for non-living things such as our home and personal belongings, all which are important for our wellbeing. There are a variety of ways in which we fulfill these fundamental human needs. However, they basically fall into two distinct categories, functional or dysfunctional, where the former is adaptive to a healthy social survival and the latter is not. In other words, we relate and care in a manner that is either good or bad for our own wellbeing.

Of course, relationships are not so black and white in a way that they can be categorized into "good" or "bad.' It is more realistic to assess relationships on a scale which can best represent where all the different aspects of a relationship fall on the scale. However, for the purposes of our discussion we are referring to relationships which fall on the more extreme ends of the scale. And these relationships are good representations of the degree to which basic human social and emotional needs are fulfilled or not.

It would be fair to say that most of us have at some point failed to assert our limits. The key is how is this a problem for you? Is it typically a challenge for you to establish your limits? Do you generally find yourself sacrificing your needs for others who can do the task themselves? You may want to ask yourself what might be your overall ability to set healthy limits with others, and how your level of ability is impacting your life, for better or worse.

Failing to establish healthy intrapersonal and interpersonal boundaries strip away a person's vital resources for a happy and healthy life. Since there are only so many hours in a day and in a person's lifetime, something's got to give. What is usually compromised is, unfortunately, what I think matters most—yourself and those you love. When you violate your own boundaries by saying yes when you mean no, it takes away time from your goals and life purpose—and time for yourself to relax, to do what you want, and to sleep and recharge. The practice of poor interpersonal boundaries takes time away from your family, your partner, your kids, and your friends. Again, violating your own personal boundaries has a negative influence in your interpersonal boundaries. Poor interpersonal boundaries in certain contexts can be harmful to some of your most valuable relationships. In general, poor boundaries takes away time and focus from what really matters to you. Does this resonate with you?

THE INTENTIONS OF OTHER PEOPLE

Regardless of what the dynamics are between two people, whether the actions of others are unfair toward you or flat-out abusive, you cannot change others. So, the ball is on your court. Often, other people are unaware of their poor relational skills, or they are attempting to meet their own goals and prioritize what is important to themselves. Hurting you is not necessarily a part of the other person's agenda. Regardless of the intent of these individuals, they are only able to take and take from you because you have not yet stopped them. In fact, you are not doing them any favors by encouraging their behavior by saying yes when you really wanted to say no.

Ultimately, you are the one to change what is not working for you, and you have two choices. Either you can continue to be a victim of the "unfairness" and "insensitivity" of others toward you, or you can take charge of yourself, as many do, and have your actions better match your thoughts in respect to "no" versus "yes." I understand it may not be an easy change for you, and yes, it is always easier said than done. However, I am not telling you that it will be easy. What I am about to tell you in the upcoming pages is that many of our interpersonal behaviors are habitual, and we can change these habits much like we can change a bad habit like nail biting. Of course, it would take intent, time and practice. One important benefit from becoming willing to learn to set healthy limits is that by doing so, you will help create an opportunity for those you please to seek to please you too.

First and foremost, change is an organic process that requires patience on your part, in addition to practice, commitment, and the willingness to learn and implement some new tools and skills. You have, most likely, been acquiring and practicing your current habits for quite a long time, and now they are second nature to you. Again, in order to replace these maladaptive habits, you need to commit to gradually stepping out of your comfort zone to practice new habits of assertiveness.

The purpose of this book is to help you improve and sustain healthier boundaries with others through self-awareness and through the insight that you will gain from what I share in these pages, as well as the tools I provide. I hope to give you an understanding of the psychological science behind your struggles to set boundaries with others, as well as the psychology behind your yeses and the intentions of those seeking your ye*ses*.

It is possible to succeed in learning to set clear limits with others. Other people have done it. This is not a special skill available only to the "privileged." In fact, it is a learned skill. You can learn most things by setting goals and practicing them until the new habits are formed. According to the neuroscientific perspective (science of the brain), the human brain is plastic, meaning it can change. Our habits are a result of learning what eventually becomes practiced thoughts and behaviors, and our brain is wired to be consistent with these behaviors. Therefore, having a flexible brain affords us the ability to learn and improve parts of the self that are not working for us. By acquiring new knowledge, changing our behaviors, and replacing our old habits, we can "rewire" or reprogram our brain to be better able to say "no," making our behaviors more adaptive to our well-being. Perfection, as always, may be impossible to achieve but we can all at least improve in this area.

2

You are Part of a System

As we have discussed in the previous chapter, an important element of healthy interpersonal boundaries is your ability to say "no" when you mean it. Saying "no" is also crucial for tending to those things that should matter most to you, such as your personal goals and time with those who are important to you. [9] When you say "yes," when you mean "no," something has got to give, and often it is going to be what is most important to you. When this happens, you are likely to become stressed and resentful of yourself and of the person you said "yes" to. This is especially true for individuals who have a history of consistently violating their interpersonal-boundaries in attempts to please others. [118, 126, 130, 131] Since practice makes perfect, it would be fair to say that these individuals are master pleasers.

It is crucial to understand that as a person, you are part of a system. Your system constitutes your internal being; how you feel about yourself; and yourself in relation to your environment, such as your home, family, pet, work, career, school, and social life, to name a few. When you say "yes" to something, your entire system shifts. This means, again, that something has to give, causing an impact on the entire system. For example, you may have less time for yourself, causing you to feel slighted. That will impact how you interact with others around you and how you perform your duties or grow. Therefore, agreeing to something has to be carefully considered so that it does not disrupt your system. The goal is to increase balance of your system, which is attained by improving your boundary skills.

Take the following example: Against her better judgment, Jacky agreed to dog-sit for her neighbors, Joe and Pat, for the duration of their two-week vacation. Jacky felt awkward about saying "no" to them because she could not give them a legitimate reason to deny their request. She thought Pat and Joe knew that she comes home early from work and likes to sit and relax in her garden. She thought her neighbors would be upset with her if she did not have a good reason to decline their request. Finally, she did not want to disappoint Joe and Pat, who spoke highly of her as the only person they trust with Ben.

She ended up feeling miserable for two weeks, having to take Ben for his three daily walks. As a result, her social life also became compromised during their vacation because she had to be home in time for Ben's bedtime walk. Jacky dislikes the commitment that pets require, and that is why she does not have one of her own. She was stressed and became resentful of her neighbors, and even more so of herself for not having said "no" to their request.

By saying "yes" to Joe and Pat, Jacky compromised her system because she agreed to do something out of her will to avoid her neighbors being upset with her. This caused her to disrupt her relaxing time after work. Having to do something she dislikes made her feel frustrated. As a result, for two weeks Jacky experienced bad feelings; stress, frustration, and resentment at home, work, and in her social life, all of which consequently disrupted her internal and external systems.

Jacky attempted to control her neighbors' reactions by agreeing to solve their problem, even though they could have found another solution for themselves. Thus, she made their problem her own. Perhaps it is fair to say that Joe and Pat's intentions were to ensure that Ben would be in good hands. Often, others' requests do not involve bad intentions toward us. Requests for favors do not always involve considering the other person, because they are often simply based on the perspective of the person asking for the favor. Since Ben is a blessing to Joe and Pat, they probably did not see him as a burden on Jacky. Perhaps they did not intend to cross boundaries by simply asking Jacky for the favor. It was up to Jacky to decline the request by gracefully saying "no" to them because, ultimately, she is the one to decide what is best for her. A more adaptive decision for Jacky would have included thanking her neighbors for their vote of trust in her, and then respectfully declining the request by saying,

> "Thank you for trusting me with Ben. I know how special he is to you, and it's flattering to me that you

both decided that I'm that special person you trust to care for him. But I'm not able to commit to watching him. Though I like him and, yes, I would take good care of him, the fact is that dog-sitting is not something I am happy doing, and with this in mind, two weeks is quite a long time. On the other hand, I would be willing to help out with Ben in case of an emergency."

By replying in this manner, Jacky does not compromise her relationship with her neighbors because: First, she acknowledged her neighbor's good appraisal of her. Second, she clarified that her "no" was unrelated to them or Ben. Rather, it was simply based on the fact that she does not like caring for pets in general. Third, her answer eliminates any future pet-sitting requests.

HOW BOUNDARY PROBLEMS EVOLVE

According to some studies, people tend to agree with the requests of others because they fear that saying "no" could cause the other person to feel upset, potentially posing a threat to their relationship.[74, 78] Humans are social beings. As such, humans are wired to bond, connect, and relate with others.[19, 31] Our first relational experiences are with our parents. From the very moment we are born, we begin to make connections with our caregivers. In fact, studies demonstrating fetal responses to environmental stimulus exist, and a growing body of research suggests that child and parental connections may actually begin forming prior to birth. [31, 109]

Forming social connections is one of the most fundamental human needs. As social beings, we place a great deal of value on our relationships, or in how we generally relate with others [18, 19, 32]. Although others might not take our "no" as badly as we think, we do have a tendency to believe that others will judge us severely if we decline a request. Even disagreeing with the opinion of others can at times be perceived as a source of tension between parties. Oftentimes, saying "no" to a request is really more of a big deal for us than for the recipient. This is because the perceived risk of losing what we greatly value (connection with and acceptance from other people) can feel threatening and scary.

During the course of our development, we have the opportunity to experience many types of relationships. These social experiences contribute to shaping who we are today and the style in which we relate to ourselves and other people. In our attempts to preserve our relationships, because of the value they hold for us, we have learned and adopted both adaptive and maladaptive thoughts and behaviors within our overall relational skills. [47, 60, 62, 65, 67]

"Adaptive" in this context refers to a person's healthy thoughts, behaviors, and other capacities that promote a positive social adjustment in life, such as assertiveness, healthy interpersonal boundaries, prosocial behaviors in general, and healthy habits. "Maladaptive" refers to thoughts and behaviors that do not promote a person's healthy social survival, meaning they do not contribute to positive outcomes in our ability to relate to ourselves and others and in our overall healthy adjustment to life.

Maladaptive thoughts and behaviors include self-victim-ization, poor interpersonal and intrapersonal boundaries, lack of assertiveness, and other unhealthy interpersonal habits. As such, saying "yes" when we mean "no" is maladaptive to a person's well being and the health of her relationships.

THE HUMAN BRAIN IS NEGATIVE

Some studies have also demonstrated that negative infor-mation weighs more heavily on the brain, due to the brain's tendency to have a negative bias in its evaluative categoriza-tion mechanism.[72] This means that the brain categorizes the input of positive and negative information in different ways. In fact, memories of our negative experiences are more eas-ily retained than positive experiences. It is believed that our brain's tendency for being more negative functions as a mecha-nism of survival. The reason for this is because when we recall bad things that happen to us, the memory of that situation is stored, and we are less likely to repeat it. For example, if you touch something hot and you burn yourself, you learn: "Whoa, that's hot, and I'm going to burn myself if I touch it again." In early development, children learn from these types of mistakes too, and they learn never to touch something that is too hot. Dogs learn in this way as well.

Additionally, negative information gets processed through the amygdala (there are actually two of them: one amygdala for each side of the brain). This is a small structure within the brain's limbic system, believed to be responsible for identify-ing perceived threats of danger. As the gatekeeper of our brain, the amygdala is believed to be fundamental in self-preservation. When we perceive a negative experience, it goes through the amygdala, which will activate at the possibility of danger. Aside from being implicated in the identification of danger, the amygdala plays an important role in mediating and controlling major affective activities, such as mood, friendship, love, and affection. These roles are made possible by its connections with other major brain structures, such as the hippocampus (which is implicated in memory) and the frontal cortex, which is implicated in higher order thinking, problem solving, judgment, and objective thought process, to name a few .[7, 40, 41, 42]

It appears that when the amygdala is activated by a perceived danger, it results in the activation of the "fight-or-flight" response, which leads the person to experience anxiety, fear, or rage in response to the event or the situation being experienced. The fight or flight response is a survival mechanism that allows for humans and other animals to respond to threats.[122, 124, 135] This mechanism was responsible for the survival of humans from predators in the savannas, where it only took a few seconds to determine whether it will eat you or you will eat it.

The amygdala seems to be activated whenever it perceives a potential for danger, and sometimes there can be false alarms, due to the activation of certain subconscious memories related to past experiences or learning. For instance, suppose you are walking alone in a dark alley, and suddenly you become very scared by the realization that someone is walking a few steps behind you. Your amygdala is activated, and you begin to go into survival mode (fight-or-flight response): you are hyper-alert, you are breathing faster, and your heart rate increases, getting you ready to fight or run. Suddenly, you realize that the person behind you is a friend, and your body then returns to normalcy. However, until this point, because you didn't know who the person was, your amygdala had alerted you of the potential danger because it was relying on the meaning of the experience. You have now stored in your memory how being alone in a dark alley could impact your safety; the sight of another person had activated this response.

Threats to our survival come in many different forms, and we assign meaning to our experiences which lead us to perceive them as being threatening or not. Sometimes there is a common perception of certain experiences as being threatening, such as swimming with sharks or skydiving. Other times, the meaning we assign to a situation is very specific to our unique experience. For example, a situation that might be scary to one person may not hold the same meaning to another. The same idea applies to the concept of pleasing, and that is why some of us please in response to the perceived threat of social rejection, while others do not perceive the same threat and therefore do not go out of their way to please.

For instance, if through my life experiences I have somehow learned to place the needs of others before mine, like Jacky (the dog-sitter) did in an earlier case example, I may become fearful whenever I risk doing the opposite—that is, considering my needs first. The idea of declining another person's request has been assigned a meaning, one of potential social disapproval.

This may then activate negative or unpleasant subconscious memories (i.e., a time in which I disappointed someone, or was abandoned by someone as a result of not complying with their wishes) [100] which would activate in me a fear of saying "no." So, our brains do not distinguish our feelings of danger or threats, whether we are fearing the sight of a tiger, public speaking or a social encounter, the brain responds in the same manner.

THE DEVELOPMENT OF PLEASING TRAITS

Studies founded in developmental psychology and attachment theories, have consistently demonstrated the impact of early experiences on the development of interpersonal patterns associated with pleasing traits. [1, 19, 20, 60] According to these studies, individuals who consistently and impulsively please others have developed these traits as survival coping mechanisms to adapt to early dysfunctional relational experiences, such as less than optimal experiences with caregivers, teachers, or other key figures within their environment. [49] In order words, humans are born with the biological capacity to experience and adapt to the environment. In early stages of life, and through experience, a person relies on environmental resources in order to ideally attain a successful (healthy) development that would prepare the individual for all future aspects of his life. This includes the relational aspects of the person. [1, 8, 10, 31, 32, 60]

This happens because in early stages of development, the brain is not fully formed, and this is when we develop the foundation for our relationships, such as the specific pattern of how we each tend to socially relate. For instance, the frontal cortex region of the brain, which is implicated in many types of superior cognitive functions, such as judgment, is not fully developed until a person's late twenties. The immature brain of young children, limits their ability to make mature judgments about what they perceive, which makes children more vulnerable to the impact of their environment.

Also, because of the limited life experiences of a child, he has not yet equipped his brain with enough frame of reference to help him make sense of his experiences. Children will adapt to their environment based on their abilities and limitations, through which early social experiences will be shaped. These early experiences will then become the foundation for newer experiences and the ongoing reorganization of the brain because of this.

If early experiences are positive, so will be their influences on development. No wonder it can be so difficult for some of us to set clear boundaries. Because our brains are wired to respond more heavily to negative experiences and we are vulnerable to early experiences of attachment, our need to belong, our irrational fear that we will lose relationships, and our worry that others will disapprove of us, it can be very difficult for some of us to say "no."[19, 101]

As you can see, unfortunately, things do not always go according to nature's plan when it comes to humans calling the shots! So, regardless of a person's biological capacity to successfully learn, grow, and relate with others, his environment can redirect his development. For instance, a person who is raised in a socially inadequate or dysfunctional, abusive and/or neglectful environment is able to learn to adapt to these circumstances by developing other coping mechanisms that will assist her to survive to the conditions of her environment. These coping mechanisms of survival will correspond to the socially inadequate conditions of the child's environment. These conditions are not prone to the successful social development of the child, because they involve the dynamics of the child's first opportunities to relate with others, and these are relationships with key figures in her life, typically her parents.

Therefore, these early poor social conditions typically lead to the development of coping mechanisms that the child naturally develops in response to her attempts to socially survive her environment. These coping mechanism or traits are usually not conducive to a healthy social adaptive survival (maladaptive). Moreover, because the child's brain is not yet fully developed, it is vulnerable to the influences of the environment. So, exposure to socially inadequate environments are likely to negatively impact the social development of young social brains. Even in cases when parents mean well, and do their best, children still have to make sense of their experiences with an immature brain, which leaves room for misperception.

These social-survival coping mechanisms also become the unique way the individual relates with others, or copes and survives future social situations. The social coping survival mechanism will serve as the frame or schema from which a person forms her relationships, and they typically consist of the inadequate style in which the person tends to relate with other people. Furthermore, the relational pattern of a person will be practiced for the rest of her life unless it is changed by the individual herself. And an example of these maladaptive coping mechanisms includes pleasing. To better illustrate this concept, let us consider the case of Jonas, a thirty-five-year-old male who has not had much luck in the arena of love.

THE CASE OF JONAS

Jonas is frustrated with his current partner and past romantic partners, whom he perceives are taking advantage of him. He complains that his partners do not do anything to contribute to the relationships. He is the one taking care of the finances, maintaining the house, buying the food, and doing the cooking. When I ask Jonas why he does so much for his partners, he claims to not to mind doing it all, but says he would like to be appreciated once in awhile.

Jonas, the oldest of five siblings, came from a dysfunctional home environment where his parents had consistent quarrels in front of the children; his mother was usually an emotional wreck—she was always sad or angry with everyone, including the children—while his father was mostly absent from the home and the kids. From an early age, Jonas began taking on a lot of his mother's responsibilities around the house and caring for his siblings in order to please her. Jonas became "parentified" (what happens when a child takes on a role of a parent).[141] Jonas took over the responsibility of his adult caregiver in order to cope with his environmental stressors.

This inappropriate coping mechanism of "caretaking to please" established the foundation for Jonas' schema of interpersonal-relationship style, which he continues to practice in the context of his romantic relationship patterns. In other words, Jonas learned to compensate for his mother's dissatisfaction, anger, emotional distance, and impaired ability to provide care and affection to Jonas and his siblings by pleasing her in an attempt to control her anger and gain love and attention from her. Jonas became the caretaker for his mother and his younger siblings. This is how he learned to show and receive love and validation. He repeats this pattern by continuing to do for others what they can do for themselves, in which case he takes over the responsibilities of his romantic partners in order to gain their love and validation. However, like his mother, his partners adapt to his care and stop appreciating Jonas because, after all, Jonas is expected to behave according to his role of romantic partner and not of a caretaker. However, Jonas perceives this dynamic from the perspective of a victim and blames his partner for not appreciating his efforts or for taking advantage of him.

Jonas' romantic partners were most likely a "maladaptive" good match for him because of their ability to easily adjust and their receptiveness to Jonas's caretaking nature. Studies have demonstrated that we tend to couple with those whose early experiences prepared them to be a match to our life perceptions.[60, 63, 65] Some say we attract others who are a match for us. Jonas's story thus illustrates this concept. In other words, his romantic partners' relational schemas include certain traits which made them prone to be in the type of relationship arrangement that they were in with Jonas.

Unfortunately, like most of us, Jonas is unable to link his current relationship patterns with his early experiences. He is lacking insight into his contribution, nor the role he plays in his relational problems, because many of the motivations that guide his relationships are subconscious.[11, 60, 61, 112] So, in order for Jonas to improve his relationships (which would improve his life) he will be required to gain awareness of the role he plays in his interactions with others. If he is able to, he might try to learn how he has become the way he is (a caretaker and pleaser). You cannot fix something you do not know is broken. So, awareness is key!

BOUNDARIES ON A CONTINUUM

For the purpose of this book, I will consider the extent to which a person is equipped with healthy boundary skills to exist on a continuum, ranging from extremely high to extremely low tendency to violate one's own boundaries. For instance, consistently or chronically engaging in pleasing behaviors, of course, would fall closer to the extremely high tendency of boundaries violation end of the continuum, because pleasing is the same as saying "yes" when you mean "no." Therefore, pleasing is dysfunctional; it is not appropriate or necessary to always feel the need to please. Instead, and ideally, the goal is to grow our capacity to say "yes" when we mean "yes." Again, pleasing sometimes is normal and a human trait. The problem is when pleasing begins to affect you, or when it is chronic, and becomes part of what defines you in the perception of others.

On the continuum of pleasers, Jonas's case would represent a moderate to more severe type of pleaser. It would be fair to say that there are different degrees of pleasers, and pleasers can be specific to a setting (e.g., either with a spouse or in the workplace). Regardless of how severe your pleasing is, you can benefit from learning about it so you can make adjustments to your boundaries, and this will only improve your well-being.

Often our parents have done the best that they can to provide us with a good upbringing. Unfortunately, even when the intentions of our parents were good, things can still go wrong. Take for instance the case of authoritarian parents who provide discipline and structure to their children, which are good things, but can be taken to the extreme. This type of parenting (e.g., "do as I say and don't ask questions") is inflexible and it serves to create followers. Our children learn to follow us and to please us, instead of developing their own autonomy and learning that they are loved unconditionally.

On the other hand, parenting styles which are too carefree and inconsistent tend to create an environment that is unstable and can result in children thinking of themselves as not important enough.

Instead, a more ideal style of parenting is the *authoritative* type. [205] This type of parenting illustrates parenting that is consistent, stable and flexible. Children, raised by an authoritative parenting style learn they are loved unconditionally for who they are. In comparison, children raised by *authoritarian* parents learn that acceptance and love is conditional to the extent that their parent's expectations of them are met. This way of gaining love and approval may become the way love and approval will be sought after in adulthood, such as with significant others or any type of relationship the person comes to develop.

Regardless of what type of home environment you had, today you can change your behaviors to improve how you relate with others. However, first we need to learn some concepts that will assist in our understanding of how we evolved to think and behave the way we each do in reference to the topic of boundaries and relationships. The first concept we will explore is perspective and perception, which is about how we come to interpret our experiences the way we do.

SELF-ESTEEM, STRESS, AND BOUNDARIES

Self-esteem is implicated in issues of boundaries, and vice versa. The effects of self-esteem and interpersonal boundaries are bidirectional; this means that one influences the other. Stress is also interconnected here. In fact, low self-esteem and high stress are both correlated with having poor boundaries. [141, 142] For instance, a person with low self-esteem tends to have very poor boundaries with themselves and others, and increased levels of stress as a result of this interaction.

Failing to set healthy boundaries causes lowering of self-esteem, which also causes stress. Healthy boundaries promote the sustainability of having higher self-esteem. This is because the better you are at setting healthy boundaries, the more self-worth you are likely to have, and higher self-worth is correlated with increased levels of self-esteem. Self-esteem and boundaries skills influence one another just as if they were located on opposite sides of a ping-pong table. Every time the ball crosses to the other side of the table, it is the result of an impact from the opposing side.

People who are more likely to practice healthier boundaries, develop higher self-appraisal, leading to the development of more self-respect and consequently higher esteem. This promotes the person's ability to better balance their individuality simultaneously with their relationships with others; thus, individuality does not need to suffer at the cost of relationships or vice versa [60, 74, 94.] Please note that this healthy balance tends to be more stable in some people than others. Regardless, it can be improved. Furthermore, because nothing is absolute, perfectly stable healthy boundaries and high self-esteem are not ever perfectly present in anyone. Both involve continuous fluctuation and require continuous maintenance.

REFLECTIVE JOURNAL EXERCISE 1

1. In what areas of your life, and in what aspects of yourself, do you believe you have the most problems with boundaries (e.g., saying "yes" when you mean "no," remaining silent instead of sharing your opinion, or asking for what you want)?

2. In which settings of your life, or in which of your relationships, do you believe you struggle mostly with boundary problems (e.g., with romantic partners, parents, coworkers, or friends)?

3. What is it about these relationships that makes it harder for you to set limits?

4. How are your boundary problems impacting your life the most (e.g., you feel tired, irritable, guilty, angry; you don't have time to work on your goals; or you feel like people don't appreciate you, or take advantage of you, or they only like you for what you do for them)?

5. Are you ever assertive? When and how? What makes you feel like you can be assertive in certain situations or with certain people, but not others?

3

Developing Healthy Boundaries in Today's World

There are only a certain number of hours in a day, and you cannot possibly do it all for yourself and everyone else. You need to be very particular about what you say "yes" to. Your "yes" needs to coincide with your *values, time, goals, wants,* and *needs.* Anytime you deviate from these five fundamental factors, you will impact your well-being, and the more you deviate, the more powerful the impact will be; the longer you practice violating your boundaries, the greater the potential side effects are, including anxiety, fatigue, and anger, to name a few. You get the picture!

It is important to keep in mind that people who have a good handle on their interpersonal boundaries are not immune to being approached by the same types of requests that pleasers receive regularly. Whether they commit to the requests or not, the difference is in how these individuals react to the requests of others, or better yet, the difference is the motivation of their response. A pleaser's motivation to please comes from a place of *need* to please and to appease. On the other hand, motivations underlying effective interpersonal boundaries instead are the result of the person's *"wanting"* to give or to do.

IT'S IMPRACTICAL TO BE A PLEASER

From a practical standpoint, it is crucial for you to make the choice to change your pleasing habits. Being a people pleaser was never practical, and it has become even more impractical in modern times. Before technology, life was different. Perhaps there was more time available to say "yes" to others since we did not have our phones and the Internet to keep us busy with work, which today we often bring home with us. Perhaps being a "pleaser" had less of an impact on a person's well-being because there was less required of us on a daily basis. Do not get me wrong: saying "yes" when we mean "no" has always been unhealthy. However, in earlier times, we had fewer external demands, as a general rule, compared to today, which also meant less pressure and the related anxiety.

Think of the time before technology, when basically all we had were typewriters to do our work. Glimpses of what we would have with today's technology were only seen on TV shows and movies like *Star Trek*, *E.T.*, or *The Jetsons*. What we have available today was once merely a fantasy of how we saw life in the future, often based on the imaginations of authors and creators of movies and books. Just 30 years ago, or so, home computers were not available to most. Internet access, email, smartphones, Skype, electronic libraries, and online schools, did not exist. Instead, we had typewriters, the postal service, brick-and-mortar libraries, and overall fewer demands.

Therefore, because of these technological limitations, there was less of an expectation for immediate replies or quick turn-around time in the completion of tasks and projects. Rather, the overall expectations of people were commensurate with the capacity they had available at that time. For instance, since information was not shared as quickly, we could only produce so much within a certain time period. So, it was not possible to send and receive documents after business hours. There was no boss with boundary issues texting all night and all weekend, and phone calls were expensive—so staying on the phone to complete extra work was a rare occurrence.

In other words, these were times when, collectively, society's expectations were more realistic compared to today. It was accepted that certain projects simply had to take longer to complete, or else required more manpower. As a society, we were also better able to focus on our work because our brains had not yet been exposed to all of the technological stimulations. Of course, there have always been certain professions that have required longer work hours. Workaholics and perfectionist pleasers have always existed, but all those individuals had were their typewriters, books, and tons of papers to keep and to move around—there were natural limits.

It is true that technology has made things more efficient because of the access and speed it offers. However, instead of using technology to more effectively accommodate the tasks we had at hand, we may have inadvertently created more work to be accommodated by our capacity to do things faster. In other words, increasingly more is expected, but there is still a person on the other side of the computer. So, now we have even more demands and higher expectations for quick turnaround because of the speed and accessibility technology offers—thus, it has become more difficult and impractical to be a pleaser in the modern day, and crucial that we learn to establish healthy boundaries.

As you can see, for the sake of time alone, it has always been impractical to please, and it can be even more impractical to please today. You have to be careful about agreeing to do things for others by taking into consideration how it will impact you beforehand. When you practice pleasing others, you are likely to place yourself in a stressful situation, which typically tends to lead to feelings of regret, resentment, and guilt.

If you'd like to begin reducing your pleasing behaviors today, you can always start by employing the "let me sleep on it" approach so you can think about a request before agreeing to it. Then, you can think of another way to help the person requesting the favor. Perhaps by providing a referral source, that the person could use instead of you, which can end up working best for everyone. For example, if a friend requires much of your time in order to help him heal from a recent breakup, you can provide him with some of your time, but you can also send him a link containing a list of therapists who specialize in this area. This way you are not taking on more than you can comfortably do.

Jerry

The concept of referring people to a different source of help other than you can be further illustrated by Jerry's case. Jerry is a thirty-five-year-old attorney working for a busy law firm. Jerry's friends frequently ask him to handle legal work for them, taking advantage of the fact that they have a friend who is an attorney. Unfortunately, Jerry is not really able to take on this additional work because he has to do it during his time off, when he could really use some rest. Additionally, the legal work is not always within his field of law, meaning Jerry has to do extra research to learn the procedure. Jerry cannot bring himself to say "no" to his friends even though they can afford to pay for an attorney of their own. Since Jerry does not want to upset his friends, he continues to suffer quietly.

After I explored this problem further with Jerry, he decided to change this behavior. He was nervous at first, as this required a way of relating that was unfamiliar to him. He got out of his comfort zone and began to refer his friends to a couple of his attorney friends. At first, he was worried about how his friends would react, but then he found himself surprised by how well they actually took it. In fact, his friends were appreciative of him for the referrals.

IS IT EVER OKAY TO PLEASE?

Implementing the word "no" into your vocabulary does not mean you should not ever help others. It is important to know when and how to help, so that helping others is done in an appropriate and realistic manner. In other words, say "yes" only when you mean it, so that giving comes from a place of wanting to give, rather than from a place of need—a need to please so that others will be happy with you, accept you, approve of you, react well to you, and give back to you.

Healthy giving requires healthy boundaries. That is correct! You must first identify your own limits before you can give. This means going with your own natural current, even it means going against the current of others. This requires identifying your own life priorities (such as those relating to personal happiness, relationships, and family, to name a few) and with that, setting your goals accordingly.

It is not a requirement for you to know exactly what your life priorities will be for the rest of your life. This might not be realistic for many, because people's needs change throughout life, according to a person's stages of development and as functions of their environment. For instance, things that once were important or of high priority to you at one point in your life, may no longer take precedence in your current stage of life. We change and we evolve. Nevertheless, whatever the priorities are that you come to identify for yourself this specific time in your life should be your focus, and you need to make sure that all your decisions are promoting of that purpose. I think you get the point. Now, what are your life priorities?

CULTURE AND PLEASING

Jerry's story obviously only represents a small scenario. There are many different types of situations where people from all walks of life are struggling with setting boundaries. I myself come from a family of many people pleasers where being nice and polite equated to striving to please everyone. It was considered selfish and rude to express your wants and needs, or to say "no" to the requests of other people. Being honest about how you felt about a situation or about others' behaviors was frowned upon. I learned to do for others regardless of how it would impact me in order to avoid being viewed as a "selfish" and "impolite" person.

Looking back today, I would not be able to function effectively if I were still lacking interpersonal-boundaries skills. I had to learn to become responsible for my own interpersonal boundaries by drawing my own lines and communicating them to others. Using interpersonal boundaries is a skill, a skill that you can learn. Culture plays a role in how we relate with the world and that includes the extent to which we tend to respect or violate personal boundaries. [25] Additionally, the role that our culture plays in influencing us is frequently subconscious, and identifying this influence will increase your self-awareness—an important aspect of self-improvement. Regardless of what the source of your boundary problem is, your cultural or gender differences, or your subconscious motivation to be liked, you can change the way you interact with others, regardless of whether or not others want to participate.

JUST AS THERE ARE THOSE WHO CANNOT SAY "NO," THERE ARE MANY WHO CAN

People who have a good handle on their interpersonal boundaries are not immune to being approached by the same types of requests that pleasers receive regularly. Whether these individuals commit to the requests or not, the difference is in how they react to these requests, or better yet, the difference is the motivation of their response. A pleaser's motivation to please comes from a place of *need* to please and to appease. On the other hand, motivations underlying effective interpersonal boundaries are the result of the person's "*wanting*" to give or to do.

Therefore, like pleasers, these individuals are also faced with requests of others, or tests to their boundaries, but they have learned to say "no" when saying "yes" would result in a maladaptive choice for them. They practice self-respect by valuing their own time. These individuals are also able to say "yes" to others without jeopardizing their own time and priorities. They know that not everything in life has the same degree of importance, and they know that saying "yes" to something will require resources (time, money, energy, and/or emotional investment).

Helen

One example of this scenario is the case of Helen, now a dedicated, forty-nine-year-old, successful public accountant, wife, daughter, and the older sister to two younger siblings. Helen had been a pleaser and fixer for her family and her company for as long as she could remember. Everyone would rely on her to pick up the slack, and she was as well-known as a pleaser and she was known for being an accountant. She was truly awesome, everyone would say, until she had a heart attack at age forty-seven.

Thankfully, Helen survived, but her pleasing personality did not. After her health incident, Helen became extremely appreciative of her second chance at life and decided to reevaluate her priorities and to implement some changes. Helen decided she would adopt the word "no" into her collection of words most frequently used. She realized that perhaps implementing this change sooner could have prevented her from the suffering the heart attack, which she believed to be the result of her being overworked and overstressed.

Today, Helen prioritizes her own life and places value on every minute of it. In other words, she does not take the time she has left in this world for granted, and is certainly not going to waste any of it out of a fear of letting people down. By shifting her perspective in this way, Helen was able to quickly change almost forty-nine years of her brain being programmed to avoid saying *"no."* So, in the context of the topic of interpersonal boundaries and pleasing, Helen no longer plays this game.

Reflection: Think of someone in your life whom you believe has the quality of practicing self-respect by appreciating their own time, yet still manages to help others at times and to maintain healthy relationships. How do you think this person is able to maintain this balance?

There are many others like Helen who have learned to place value on their time. These people know that in order to stay focused and to take care of themselves, their loved ones, and to attain their own life goals, they need to say "no" to anything that will take time away from getting closer to these goals. They realize that the time they have in life all comes down to simple adding and subtracting, and so the more they take on, the less time is left to do the things that are important to them. These individuals decide what matters most to them, and they protect this by eliminating what does not. I call it *streamlining*. This practice does not work for pleasers because the life paths of pleasers are often being interrupted or redirected by the needs of other people.

THE GOOD NEWS

We are creatures of habit. As such, we have habituated ourselves to be pleasers and have habituated others to be the recipients of our pleasing. However, you can learn new skills and improve your interpersonal effectiveness. You can make a decision to change and stick to the process until you do. When you transform, others will, in time, adjust to the *new* you. Your modification will be incremental, and because change requires the introduction of something new, it will require a psychological adjustment. This is also how others will adapt in their response to you. After a while, the old you with the old ways will be forgotten, and so will the old ways of others in response to you. *No one needs to lose for you to win.*

THE CASE OF ALICE

Alice's boyfriend demanded more of her time when she was already stretched thin with work deadlines and taking care of her children during the busy back-to-school week. She complied with Dave's requests anyway, despite the negative impact this was having on her well-being and on *her whole life.*

This scenario happens to be common for many individuals who irrationally react to the needs of others. In Alice's situation, she consistently finds ways to justify behaviors to please Dave. Subconsciously, her motivations were related to her fear of upsetting Dave to a point that he would find her inadequate to be his girlfriend and end up leaving her—very catastrophic in nature, wouldn't you agree? Alice would not only please Dave, but she would please and fix everything for her children, her parents, her boss, her friends, and her past boyfriends.

Like Alice, when you do things for others that are inconsistent with what you want or can do, it is as if you were to let someone else take the driver's seat in your life. You're the only one who knows exactly where you want to go, and so you must be the one driving. Alice first needed to become aware of what was not working (or not working effectively) for her, and then she was able to change her attitude toward herself by deciding to commit to treating herself with respect and prioritizing her own needs. Alice worked to change her habit of letting others determine how she spent her time, which led her boyfriend, Dave, to change his perception of her (as the pleaser) and to habituate to her changes. Alice soon realized that she would have it no other way.

REFLECTIVE JOURNAL EXERCISE 2

Does Alice's story resonate with you or anyone you know? Have you prioritized your needs today?

4

Are you Aware of Your Own Boundary Issues?

Frequently, we are not aware of our maladaptive pleasing traits. This simply means we do not always know the role we play in the dynamics of our relationships or that we handle certain situations in a way that may be detrimental. Also, people are not always aware of how their choices impact the flow of their lives—for example, how poor interpersonal boundaries interfere with what matters most to them, because this lack of awareness interferes with effectively prioritizing what they value the most. So, awareness is key here.

In order for interpersonal boundaries to improve, it is also important for the person to:

- Become aware of his strengths and limitations in this area and how it is impacting his life.
- Assess how your life could be different with the implementation of effective interpersonal boundaries.

- Observe how far back you can remember having been a pleaser for others, as this can be effective in cultivating deeper insights to assist in the process of developing self-awareness.
- Assess your own obstacles, such as what fears or motivations are preventing you from practicing better interpersonal boundaries, is key.
- Learn new relational skills involving effective boundaries, and assertiveness with others will help you replace old habits with new ones.
- Get out of your comfort zone by actually implementing new behaviors, such as saying "no" when needed, and consistently practicing these new behaviors until they become habits.

WHAT'S NEXT FOR YOU?

If you are reading this book, you most likely desire to improve your ability to set healthy interpersonal boundaries with others in one or more settings of your life (such as in your romantic life, work relationships, and/or friendships). Ultimately, you need to ask yourself if you really want to change the way you treat yourself in relation to others, and if you value your time and energy.

You might also want to ask yourself what would be the advantages and disadvantages of changing, from consistently placing the needs of others before your own, to prioritizing your own needs first. Perhaps you subconsciously feel that being a victim has worked for you, maladaptively of course, and so you may perceive making this change as causing a loss of whatever benefit this victimhood was giving you. For instance, you derive some degree of comfort from violating your needs maybe because this is the way you have learned and practiced relating to others (old tricks of an old dog). However, you might want to once again consider the old saying "Practice makes perfect!" Do you really want to continue being perfect when it comes to being a pleaser?

YOUR DEFAULT SETTING

It is important to remember that learning new behaviors does take practice. You did not come to be the way you are overnight. The way you constantly think and behave (and the interaction it had with your genetic predispositions and life experiences) has evolved into your own natural tendencies. For example, some people tend to generally have a more positive outlook on life, and that includes holding a positive image of themselves, while others are generally less positive. These natural overall tendencies unique to the individual occur by "default" in a person. In other words, if I am, by default, a pessimistic person, then I will have pessimistic reactions to situations, by default.

Think of the nature of your overall perspective as the default setting by which your relationships will all be based on, and that will only become reinforced with more practice.[5,7,30,125] Your default setting is like the homepage you have set for your internet browser. It is the nature of your overall perspective and what typically becomes activated in you, or your tendency to react (internally and externally) in particular ways—by default.

A general example would be, if you have low self-esteem, it is likely that your default setting has been shaped around the overall less optimal view you hold of yourself. This would cause you to automatically have negative reactions to situations you perceive as a violation to your worth. For instance, you might take a comment personally, and feel upset, inadequate or worthless, even if the comment was not directed at you.

Your default setting also includes your default coping mechanism, which consists of the internal coping tools you have developed along the way to deal with the difficult situations that your immature brain sought to make sense of when you were a child. These default mechanisms are activated on demand by your new experiences or thoughts. So, the nature of how you tend to cope with life relies on the nature of your overall general vantage point and attitude towards life, such as whether you are generally optimistic, pessimistic, resentful, content, or generally feel worthy, to name a few.

Consistently saying "yes" when you mean "no" is a type of maladaptive mechanism that becomes activated based on the nature of your default setting and your interaction with a given situation (*who, what,* and *when*). On the other hand, if your default setting tends to be more positive and adaptive to your well-being, so will your default mechanisms. Being able to establish and maintain healthy boundaries with yourself and other people, is an example of a healthy default mechanism that, in response to a specific situation, becomes activated according to the nature of your overall positive default setting. In other words, a person's overall pre-dispositions to react internally and behaviorally to what she perceives, such as in the context of social situations, reflects the degree of her general social competence.

Generally speaking, the way you perceive your internal and external environment (your thought and your relationships) will play a role in the activation of your default setting. Both your thoughts and experiences will activate your state of being, your behaviors, and the tools you use in response to this activation (what you do, and how you cope). This process, or way of responding to the environmental stimuli, is ongoing, and the way people tend to respond reinforces their current perception of themselves, their perception of other people, and of their life in general—thus continually supporting similar beliefs and behaviors. [117, 125, 127]

Your overall life perspective is the lens through which you view yourself and others, as well as the lens that allows you to experience your past and present. It has evolved over time and is shaped by your life experiences. Your perspective can also be referred to as your vantage point, or point of view. Perception on the other hand is the act of experiencing what you see though your lens (perspective). More specifically, perception is how you interpret experiences, and these interpretations are based on your overall point of view. So, to perceive is to see or experience a situation in a way that is unique to you. This is because your perception is based on the unique lens through which you view the situation at hand (your perspective).

Your perception of yourself and others impacts your experiences, such as the way you think, feel, and behave, as well as the quality of your relationships, because again, it is the lens through which you view yourself and the world. Perspective and perception are powerful concepts because they underlie all that we experience; who we are (what we think, feel, and do with ourselves and others). While your perception shapes the experiences in your life, your experiences further shape your *perspective*

Another term for "perspective" is "paradigm." You can change your perspective or you can shift a paradigm. Both mean the same thing, that is, you can change the way you view a situation and your life by changing the angle which you view it from (or by changing the lenses which you view it through).

This concept is also well demonstrated in the history of society and by the sciences, where collectively major paradigm shifts have been evident. For instance, women's rights are the result of a major change of perspective about the place and value of women in society. The idea of a flat versus a spherical-shaped planet Earth also demonstrates a major paradigm shift in science. If we think hard, we might remember a time when we may have accomplished a paradigm shift about an incident or an old belief about ourselves, another person, or a situation, resulting in our ability to see things differently now. This describes a shift in paradigm. The way we relate to other people including our interpersonal boundaries was shaped by learning and interpretation of our earlier experiences, and we can further change how you interpret these experiences.

A person's overall perception only changes with a change in the person's' overall perspective. For example, interrupting the pattern of being generally sensitive to the feedback of others and generally reacting with passive aggression would require changing aspects of the person's perspective for that to be a change in the way she comes to perceive feedback from others, thus changing the meaning she decides to assign to feedback she receives from others.

To reiterate, a person's default setting consists of what is typically activated in the person as a result of how he perceives or interprets experiences, such as the overall types if reactions which are automatically activated in the person in her interaction with others. Consistent violation of self-boundaries (when pleasing is habit) suggests an overall default setting, consisting of an underlying motivation for placing the needs of others before your own, which again, is not an adaptive mechanism [34, 127, 138, 131, 140].

HOW DO WE DEVELOP OUR PERSPECTIVE?

A person's perspective evolves over time and it is formed as a result of how each unique individual process, assimilates, or makes sense of each moment of his or her life experiences. Your beliefs of yourself have by now evolved into a system of schemas, or frames of references, which shape the lens through which you view yourself, the world, and yourself in relation to the world. For instance, your schemas of relationships can either be adaptive to your well-being or not (e.g., *"I knew it! I can't trust anyone to do things for me!"* Or *"Men are all jerks!"*).

This may be because of how you have lived and the way you have been programed to perceive your world. We have covered this in our earlier discussion about how our coping survival mechanisms develop. So, you can see how our coping survival mechanisms will match our perceptions.

Consistently placing the needs of others before your own is an example of a mechanism people often adopt as a result of what they have taken away from earlier life experiences with others. From this information, we form our schemas or our references for new experiences, with which we will perceive new situations. Our social coping survival mechanisms develop from our attempts to survive earlier social experiences. So, whatever the interpretations of our new social experiences are (how we perceive it), we will adapt to it by implementing the social mechanisms we have developed to cope and survive in other social experiences that have elicited similar feelings in us, such as fears, anxieties, and anger. So, these become the tools (good or bad) that are used when you respond or interact with other people.

OBJECTIVE VERSUS SUBJECTIVE PERCEPTION

We will further examine the concept of perception in two ways. First, an experience can be objective, referring to what is actually taking place at the given moment, such as when it is raining, or snowing outside. These occurrences are objective situations. In other words, everyone can agree that it is currently raining outside. However, the way we each experience these same scenarios is based on our unique perception of these experiences. For instance, I might perceive a rainy day as depressing, whereas you might perceive it as a relaxing and cozy day. So, the meaning you and I have assigned to the experience of a rainy day is subjective to our perception. Two people with two different interpretations of the same situation, and this can frequently be a source of a dysfunctional dynamic.

We perceive experiences from the conscious and subconscious levels (aware or unawareness). So, when we "misinterpret" something, it is the result of seeing what we believe is there (e.g., people don't like me) based on our own perception and our underlying belief system (in this case, low self-worth) shaped the lens that we use to interpret that people do not like us in our experiences with them.

The practice of self-violation of boundaries is frequently operated from an underlying irrational and subconscious interpretation of a situation. For example, if I believe that if I say no to your request you will abandon me, this belief is subjective to my own perception. I do not objectively know that it is necessary true that you will leave me if I don't do what you want. So, my behaviors are than shaped by my subjective beliefs. This is why even when I want to say no, I might say yes because my subjective underlying belief system is influencing my decisions.

CHANGING THE DEFAULT SETTING

It is necessary to change how we interpret experiences to change our predispositions to react in certain ways (default setting). This is accomplished by attempting to view a situation from a different vantage point, which can help us to consider other possibilities of what might be actually taking place. Instead you might consider the possibility that the behavior of the other person towards you could be unrelated to you. For example, the other person might be experiencing personal problems, which may be impacting the way he is interacting with you.

Individuals who naturally have a generally positive disposition to life (who are equipped with a healthy coping mechanism by default), tend to be better able to take bad situations less seriously. Their perception has been framed around more optimism. However, if you are not naturally more inclined to optimism, you can change your overall perception through learning. For instance, see the case of Kathy a thirty-six-year-old married high-school teacher, who could replace her negative default coping mechanisms with adaptive ones. This has reshaped her perception, which in turn has impacted the dynamics of her entire life.

Kathy

To make Kathy's (extremely) long story short, she basically came from a complicated upbringing involving childhood abuse. Kathy's perception of self and the world had been very much shaped by her past experiences, which did not feel good to her. Kathy had decided to work on herself, and she had been doing so for many years, which included actual treatment with a therapist and other self-help approaches. Over the years, Kathy was finally able to learn and accept that despite all the bad things that had happened to her, the world was not out to get her and that what happened in her past had nothing to do with her. With this new angle of perception, she developed other more adaptive survival mechanisms, which enabled her to have more positive relationships.

Kathy had become more receptive to the constructive feedback from others. She has learned to see them as areas she could further improve. She has also learned to see these "improvement-needed areas" in context with all the other positive and already working aspects of herself. Kathy's change in perception has allowed her to see herself as "good enough" in so many ways that when she receives feedback reflecting a "lack of" something, she is actually glad to have this brought to her attention so that she can now work on it. This change in mindset impacted how Kathy now perceives feedback from others as advantageous to her growth instead of a threat to her worth.

These new and more adaptive coping mechanisms that Kathy now possesses have become interwoven in all aspects of her life (in the same way as her old less adaptive coping survival mechanisms were), and this includes establishing limits with others. This is because she has become more self-attuned as a result of her personal transformation. Self-attunement involves gaining self-awareness (learning about oneself or being more in touch with yourself), which includes becoming aware of how the ways we perceive, feel and behave play a role in our interactions with others, as well as how and why other people impact us. Once this is explored, the person, in this case Kathy, can make conscious decisions about what types of thoughts she wants to focus on and the types of behaviors she will choose to practice, including what she says "yes" and "no" to.

Kathy today also understands that this process is non-negotiable when it comes to making personal changes, and at times the process will take longer than other times. She also understands that, as life unfolds, new needs arise, and so do the adjustments we must make to accommodate these needs. This is why she continues to work on herself as part of her way of life, and I encourage this practice, as much as your doctor encourages the practice of daily physical activity.

Reflection: Have you been in a situation with other people where each person ended up walking away with completely different experiences? Maybe one of you felt the interaction with the other person to be insulting, and the other could not disagree with you more? This is an example of two different representations of the same situation, or two different perspectives.

WHAT IS EXPECTED OF YOU?

Hopefully, you remember reading in chapter 2 that *you are part of a system*. Your system constitutes your internal being, how you feel about yourself, and yourself in relation to your environment (in your home, with your family and pet, at work, in your career, at school, and in your social life, to name a few). When you say "yes" to something, your entire system will shift. That means something has to give, causing an impact in the entire system. The same phenomenon happens when instead you say "no" to others or to situations. When saying "no" is going to protect your well-being and the wellbeing of others around you, the impact it will have in your system is going to be more positive. Saying "no" when you need to also frees you up to say "yes" when it's most important to you and to the people and things that really matter.

The irony is that by protecting your well-being, you can be more available to others. Your relationships become more meaningful and sustainable because you are operating from a place of wanting rather than from a place of need. I am suggesting that you capitalize on your need to please in a way that is adaptive to you and those around you by utilizing it as a motivation to change. The idea is that by improving your intrapersonal and interpersonal competence, others will also benefit. In other words, when you are well, others around you will also be well. Again, understanding why it is important to have healthy boundaries is the first step. The second step consist of developing awareness of where your own problems with boundaries came from. Third, in order to commit to the process of change, you will be required to take yourself out of your comfort zone.

Now, this is that time when saying "yes" would be appropriate and very much needed for the sake of your well-being and the wellbeing of others around you. Are you willing to feel uncomfortable for a good cause? If your answer to this question is "yes," then read on...

5

The Biology of Experience

Experience is not just based on what is happening in your external environment. We also have an internal reaction that makes up part of our experience. The internal reaction is comprised of the physiological response which we experience as feelings, emotions and sensations that are the result of the external experience. How a person perceives a given situation will depend on how they experience it both externally and internally. This means that when you experience a pleasant social situation, you are likely to activate associated feelings of safety and worthiness, as well as the corresponding physiology, such as serotonin and oxytocin, which are two feel-good chemicals implicated in mood regulation and human relationships. These among other factors comprise an internal response. Something similar happens when your experiences are unpleasant, such as the activation of feelings of resentment and fear, which implicates the fight-or-flight response (e.g., fear for your life or of social rejection) discussed earlier in chapter 1, which initiates the secretion of stress related hormones, and the activation of the sympathetic nervous system. [7, 30, 40, 42, 55, 106]

It is important to remember that our experiences dictate the specific physiological and emotional response we will be required to endure. However, we can choose more adaptive responses instead of behaving reactively to our experiences, such as in the earlier example of Jonas' case. Again, attempting to view the situation from a different vantage point is a good way to redirect our natural tendency (default) of responding to experiences.

On a side note, by making an effort of redirecting the way we respond to the world, we are redirecting the course of our health. This is well illustrated by the concept of epigenetics, which considers the interaction of gene expression and the environment. According to this discipline, we have the capacity to influence gene expression in response to our experiences. So, good experiences are correlated with good biology, good emotions, and overall well-being, causing a positive impact in your entire system. Pleasing causes stress and burnout because of the burden it places on the individual and relationships, and when experienced by a person, these pleasing symptoms will elicit a matching physiology in response.

IMPLICATION OF NATURE VERSUS NURTURE IN PLEASING

An infant's unique personality at birth equips her individual capacity or predisposition to interact with her environment, and this includes how she processes these new experiences. Thus, a person's experiences are the result of and interaction of her biological predispositions and her interactions with the environment. To better illustrate this, biologically, we are born with the capacity to perceive and respond to what we perceive. To perceive something (e.g., a situation) is to experience it, and we begin to experience our environment at birth. So, perception is implicated in our development in a very big way.

A child perceives her environment and becomes motivated with the intent to explore it. She then begins to activate other parts of her brain, nervous system, and motor skills in response to her eagerness to explore what is being experienced. This results in stimulating brain development to equip her to attain her developmental milestones, such as, walking for the first time, as well as the development of her social brain. This interaction with her environment is also facilitated by her interpretation of her own experiences (how she perceives it), which is responsible for shaping her early relational schemas (her reference bank).

Once again, through our ability to perceive, we experience and interpret the world, which begins even prior to birth. The interpretation and shaping of the child's relational schemas becomes reinforced with new experiences. Experiences resulted from the child's interactions with key figures begins to establish the way she relates to others in future relationships, and that includes the kind of intrapersonal or interpersonal boundaries she will end up adopting.

Children born in the same environment as their siblings, may perceive their surroundings uniquely different from one another. This may be because of the influence of the biological component (nature) of what shapes personality—there are no two people alike. For example, a good-natured child, or one with socially receptive predispositions, should, if all goes well in his or her environment, elicit responses from his primary caregiver consistent with his nature. [80] The same would happen with a child whose personality is more anxious, whose parental response would also be consistent with his or her anxious nature. So, good natured versus anxious natured parents are likely to elicit a matching response from their infant. This bidirectional relationship where the child impacts his environment and, the child's environment impacts the child, can again be illustrated by the concept of the ping-pong-table presented in chapter 2, where one player impacts the other. This kind of co-creation of perception leads to how we end up experiencing life and continue to create new experiences with ourselves and others.

In summary, our experiences shape perspective (the lenses which we interpret life) of ourselves and life in general, and vice versa, and this begins in the very first stages of a person's life. Our perception is unique to us and it evolves from what we elicit from others and what others elicit from us. It is a bidirectional interaction where A impacts B, and B impacts A. Two people deal with the same situation in unique ways based on each person's perception of the situation. In other words, the same problem can affect two individuals in very unique ways. Do you remember the earlier example of a rainy day?

THE IMPLICATION OF SELF-PERCEPTION & SELF-CONCEPT ON BOUNDARY

As it was more or less included in the explanation earlier, our perception is not only limited to the environment and the people in it. Our perception also implicates how we view or interpret ourselves, referred to as *our self-perception*. As part of our general perception, our self-perception is specific to our capacity to interpret ourselves. Our self-concept is the frame or lens which we view ourselves through, which has also evolved over time, resulting from the meanings we have assigned to our life experiences as it relates to oneself.

In other words, self-perception is how we interpret experiences about ourselves and self-concept is the point of reference or frame through which we perceive ourselves. Self-concept is shaped over time from earlier experiences. Our perception or interpretations of these experiences have lead us to shape our self-concept, that is to view ourselves in a certain way compared to other people, or to assign a worth to ourselves. [137]

The ping-pong-table concept presented earlier, can also be applied to illustrate the concept of self-perception and self-concept. For instance, your positive self-perception will elicit more positive experiences, which will have a positive impact in shaping your self-concept (how you view yourself). In turn, your negative self-perception will most likely negatively influence the way you view yourself. So, you will continue to look for evidence to support the negative belief system you hold of yourself (e.g., "I am not worthy"). One way in which this happens is through interpreting the behaviors of other people as directed at you because of your perception of lack of worth. A person who holds a negative self-concept tends to interpret from that frame, even simple situations involving other people such as, of someone forgetting to call them. For example, *"I knew Kathy wouldn't call me! She did call Jane though! But again, can't blame Kathy for picking Jane over me, Jane is smart and fun to be around. People don't really want to be around me if they have a choice."*

Within our self-concept we have formed schemas or categories. For instance, we have schemas that represent how we view our own intellectual capacity in different areas of our lives, and schemas for how we view our own physical attractiveness, among others. Our schemas provide us with more specific point of reference related to how we view different aspects of ourselves in relation to other people.

How you see yourself or your self-concept also serves as a point of reference in opportunities for new experiences. For instance, *"Am I good enough for that person to date me? Am I good enough for that promotion? Am I confident about the good work I have contributed?"* Our self-concept is formed as a consequence of how we have perceived ourselves (the meanings we have taken from our experiences as it relates to us).

Therefore, your overall self-concept, implicates your confidence, the self-concept of your intellectual capacity or smart you view yourself, your level of self-importance, to name a few. It is based on the lens through which you see yourself that you think others see you, too.

Generally speaking, a person's self-concept is largely comprised of low-self-worth-prone qualities and tend to typically result in experiences involving feelings of insecurity and low esteem, such as "I always mess up, I'm not smart, I'm not attractive," and these feeling likely contribute to the cycle of a person's negative interpretation of her experiences. [137]

On the other hand, a person's self-concept mostly comprised of healthy self-worth is likely to provide her with qualities prone to more positive interpretations of her experiences. Generally speaking, the more you perceive yourself positively, the more positive your self-concept tend to be, as will your overall level of confidence, self-esteem, and your overall capacity to socially adapt.

Our perceptions are subjective because they are based on our interpretation, or the meanings we have assigned to our life experiences. Often our subjectivity tends to guide us to assume as facts, aspects of a situation that are not necessarily accurate. For example, we tend to assume what others might be thinking of us. Our assumptions based on our perception of another person are often incorrect because they lack objective evidence. This occurs with all of us, pleasers or non-pleasers. A pleaser's tendency to sacrifice himself for the benefit of another tends to be linked to schemas comprised of qualities related to a learned sense of "low" self-worth. This attributes to pleasers perceiving themselves as lacking certain qualities, and learning specific compensating traits for their survival, that is "to please" as a way to attain self-worth, which is not necessarily adaptive.

Unfortunately, these survival mechanisms that evolve from most pleaser's negative self-perception provide opportunities for pleasers to put their own needs last. This is because the core of these mechanisms constitutes a person's attempt to compensate for his or her perceived inadequacies. For example, "I don't have anything to offer you, but if I don't say no to you,

you will accept me." Often, this attempt to compensate causes the person to become other-focused, meaning the individual develops a tendency to place the needs of others first, and this requires that his focus be mostly oriented toward other people rather than on himself.

THE IMPLICATION OF UPBRINGING ON PLEASING

Typically, chronic pleasing traits can be seen in adults who were once children of emotionally unavailable or emotionally unstable parents. Children of parents who were ill could develop certain traits as a result of having to care for the emotional needs of the parent or of their siblings, resulting in these children developing a relational framework consisting of behavior patterns involving others first.

This is also seen in adults who were children of parents who maintained inflexible and high standards for their children. These parents meant well; however, their inflexibility led their children to seek perfection in order to please their parents, and because attaining such perfection is impossible, these children never really experienced their parents' contentment toward them. Instead, these children became fulfilled with the *expectation* of making their parents happy (the habit of pleasing is really the expectations involved in the process of trying to please, because pleasing others is difficult). This led these children to strive to succeed at higher and higher levels, but they had their parents as the primary motivator. That is, the "other."

This ongoing attempt at perfection with the purpose of other-pleasing becomes the mechanism which the person comes to bring into his or her adult life. There are many other examples of how and why these maladaptive traits develop; each individual has his or her unique story to tell. But the content of the story is not as important as the quality of the experience. It is important for children to learn to balance a focus on themselves as the individual and on others. The closer we are able to attain this balance, The more likely are quality social experiences. The better the quality of the experience, the better is the potential life outcome of the adult.

Irene

The case of Irene, a forty-five-year-old woman, illustrates another example of early inadequate experiences that contribute in shaping our social brains. During her childhood development, her father was emotionally and physically absent, and her mother was emotionally immature. She perceived Irene, although she was her child, as her best friend, and she relied heavily upon Irene for emotional support. As a child, Irene was exposed to more developmentally inappropriate information than she was able to process.

Irene also learned that in order be loved, she had to emotionally take care of others. Irene's perception was shaped by her earlier relationships with her parents, and has since been adopted in her future relationships with others. Irene also suffers from low self-worth, and she keeps making the same mistakes in her relationships. Irene struggles with interpersonal boundaries, where she feels her romantic partners and friends take advantage of her. As a pleaser to her mother, Irene formed her perception out of fear of being disapproved of and the need to be appreciated. This is how she learned to bond and to love.

The underdeveloped child's brain is vulnerable. It lacks judgment and it is under-equipped with memories and learning that serve as points of reference the child can use in his attempts to make sense of his new experiences. Therefore, exposing his to inadequate experiences impacts the shaping of his brain. Again, our earliest relational experiences shape the way we view our self and others, and it equips us to relate in future relationships.

The meaning we have assigned to the experiences of our earlier interactions with others form the frame which we perceive ourselves and our relationships, and this continues to be reinforced as we continue to interact in our relationships. On the other hand, when our positive self-concept guides our prior experiences, our future relational experiences will continue to reinforce what we learned, in which case, we feel that we are good enough. Understanding this concept is crucial in understanding our relationships with others, and the good news is, you can gradually change how you perceive yourself, and your overall self-concept.

ASSUMPTIONS ARE JUST AS DANGEROUS AS PERCEPTION

Perception is our unique interpretation of what we experience, and assumptions are what we deduce is happening based on our interpretation and not necessary resulting from concrete facts. Our overall experiences in relation to ourselves, others, and the world as a whole are impacted by our perception. Again, because our perception is subjective, we frequently make incorrect assumptions about the perceived intentions of others toward us. Often, we do not realize that our initial assumptions were incorrect. This can be problematic because we make inferences about others or situations based on zero evidence to back it up, and it is based on these assumptions that we often act.

Take the case of Sally, a thirty-year-old computer analyst, for example. Sally's assessment of the general demeanor of her coworker Jane, led Sally to formulate the assumption that Jane thought of her as inferior. Sally would read her coworker Jane's friendliness with all their other coworkers, but not with Sally, as Jane's disinterest in her because of Sally's self-perceived "inferiority." Later, Sally was placed on a project with Jane, when she learned that Jane was actually a shy person, and she was also reading Sally's distance as lack of interest in her. So, Jane too was lacking confidence to approach Sally. In other words, both individuals were struggling with the same fears and were assuming the opposite intentions of one another. Sally and her Jane's views of each other were based on their own insecurities about themselves. So, their perception was being influenced by their underlying schemas of self-concept.

As you can see, our perception can frequently cause problems in how we relate to others. There are times that you assume others come from a place of disregard toward you, in that they request so much of you. Often the person does not have the intention to abuse you. Instead, the person may have been habituated to your accommodations of his or her past requests, so they have learned your limits, or lack thereof. Additionally, it is also important to consider that people have their own conscious and subconscious objectives in mind and cannot be in tune with your boundaries, unless you make these clear. After all, it is your job to be in tune with your own needs and communicate that to others whenever appropriate and necessary.

One effective way to reduce the possibility of being influenced by our assumptions (or misassumptions) is to ask yourself if you have evidence of what you are thinking is in fact true. You can also simply ask the other person for clarification when possible. This can be done by adopting "I" statements to express how we feel or perceive a specific situation. For instance, you can say, "*I feel* I am not welcome here; am I correct about my assumptions?" You can also use "it seems" in order to address your perception of a situation without jumping into conclusions and formulating incorrect assumptions. For example, you can say, "*It seems* my presence is causing you some degree of discomfort. Am I correct in my assumptions?"

Both approaches are tools you can use to clarify your doubts about a situation while taking responsibility for owning your own perception. In other words, you are saying that this is how you see, feel, and so on, instead of assuming what is or is not, and/or attempting to gain clarification in an accusatory manner such as "*You don't* want me here" instead of "*You seem* uncomfortable with me being here, am I correct about my perception?" As you can see, there are different ways to deal with our perception. Another way to clarify miscommunication is by paraphrasing what was said by the other person. In other words, you repeat to the person what you have heard he or she say to you (e.g., "so, what I hear you saying is…")

I use the following concept with my clients to illustrate how our assumptions influence our relationships: When you assume something about a person or a situation, it is the same as if you were a screenwriter and director who failed to share the script of your screenplay with the participating actors. You then star in all the parts, and begin to play the movie over and over in your head. Your screenplay ends up being so good, and as an actor, you do such a great job, that you become convinced the movie is real and those playing the parts are in reality participating in the plot.

Remember that you will elicit an emotion and a physiology corresponding to your internal or external experiences. A thought that you hold comprises an internal experience, and if your screenplay is eliciting of positive feelings, you are in good shape. However, often this is not the case, and instead your incorrect assumptions about a person or a situation, your screenplay will cause you a great deal of suffering.

BOUNDARIES AND PERCEPTION

Why do we act against our will? What is the reason for sacrificing ourselves to please another person in saying "yes" when we actually mean "no?" As we have discussed, our social brains are shaped through development, and so are our individual tendencies to socialize in unique ways. [137] An individual tendency to self-violate his boundaries is part of his relational style. He has learned to sacrifice himself as a means to socially succeed. And as we have already established, self-sacrifice is not an adaptive means of social competence.

Over time of consistent practicing, pleasing skills have become embedded in you. Over time pleasing has also contributed to shaping your belief system and your schemas of self-concept, which impact how you perceive yourself and the world around you. Somewhere along the way, you learned to put the needs of others before yours. For example, you learned to avoid upsetting others so they would continue liking you. You fear rejection, so you say "yes." You say "yes" because you fear disapproval from others or even abandonment.

However, whatever the underlying root cause of your pleasing is, you are attempting to control the reaction of others at any cost, even if that means losing or hurting what may be most important to you, such as your time, your family, and yourself.

The source of power to solutions for your unique problems resides within yourself. Oftentimes, your consistent and perceived unappreciated pleasing will have you believe that your problems are caused by others, and if only the other person would change his or her behavior (have more regard for you), then things would be okay. Thus, you feel a complete lack of control in the situation.

Both through my work and personal life, I have observed and learned about several common faulty thought processes and behavioral themes among individuals who cannot set healthy interpersonal limits. For instance, these individuals have a tendency to do the following:

1. They feel victimized by others ("Why does he do this to me?" "Why me?").
2. They perceive that they lack power and control to stop others, and so they stay in the situation, regardless of their dissatisfaction and suffering.
3. They have low self-worth, and as a result, have developed irrational thinking, such as, *"If I were better (smarter, prettier, richer, etc.), this would not have happened to me,"* or *"If this were the case, that person would have greater respect for me."*
4. They have developed the belief that bad things happen to them because of "bad luck.
5. Finally, sometimes the person cannot seem to cut ties completely with unhealthy relationships that are draining and one-sided. As a result, fatigue and burnout, lead to resentment and anger. These themes represent the person's overall self-perception and thus, after a while, become deeply ingrained in the core of a person.

As we have been covering, early interpersonal experiences provide us with a life perspective and the *internal working model* for how we relate with others.[101, 137] These early experiences which are expected to equip us with adequate social adaptations skills, end up failing us. Frequently and unintentionally our primary caregivers end up teaching us skills otherwise adaptive to our social competence. And the process includes developing an overall negative belief system which includes a negative perception and appraisal of self. This underlying belief system also influences the health of our relationships, reinforcing our negative self-perception, and perpetuating the maladaptive-pattern of pleasing. Given this concept, it is not surprising for our self-esteem to be impacted, further influencing future unhealthy pleasing patterns of relationship.

If you happen to be a pleaser you might know that the longer you please, the more tired you become. Loss of identity, fatigue and burnout are a typical complaint: "I don't know who I am anymore," "I'm tired of relationships," "I just want to be alone," "I don't care anymore," "I'd rather continue to do whatever he wants until... I don't know what," "I'm not arguing anymore," "I don't care," "I only have peace when I'm at work. Then, I try to occupy my time after work with cleaning the house," "I'll go to bed early, and I never have to deal with him." Handling burnout in this manner is in itself not adaptive, as it leads to a never-ending reinforcement of the poor self-concept, more exhaustion, and eventually resentment and anger.

THE CONCEPT OF LOCUS OF CONTROL AND BOUNDARIES

The term "locus of control" refers to the source of a person's operational power[202.] For instance, blaming other people for how you feel is redirecting responsibility to another, as well as giving your power away to another. People who have poor boundary issues tend to attribute what happens to them to forces outside of their control. People operate from an internal or external locus of control, where "internal locus" refers to a person's tendencies to take responsibility for his or her own choices and behaviors. The person is then operating from the perspective of free will. From this view, a person understands that she is ultimately the one to choose her own destiny based on the variables that are within her or her control.

When a person attributes her experiences and destiny to her own free will, she is operating from her internal locus of control. For instance, when you operate from your internal locus of control, you might say that you find a person's actions irritating, instead of accusing the person of irritating you. The latter illustrates external locus of control. When a person operates from this vantage point, she makes attributions to others and circumstances outside of her control, in order to justify her own state of being. When we operate from an external locus of control, we experience a perceived lack of control because something or someone was the cause of our bad feelings or misfortune. For example, you blame the weather for your mood. You blame your husband for not making you happy. You blame your mother for your lack of success. You blame God for having made you poor, and so forth. n all these examples, *you* are the "victim!"

Poor interpersonal boundaries tend to operate from an external locus because the person gives up her power to another when she says, "yes" against her will. Doing for others against one's own will tends to create unrealistic expectations of others to return appreciation for the favor. Since the behaviors of other people are outside of our control, placing ourselves in the position of expecting a return for what we do for others, is the same as giving up control, and "victims" do not have control. This externalization of power and control (e.g., "I always do for you and you don't appreciate it!") also illustrates an external locus of control that pleasers tend to operate from.

Internal or external locus of control does not only apply to negative attributions, such as bad feelings or poor behavior choices. It actually encompasses all types of different scenarios. For instance, a person who operates from an external locus of control would attribute a raise in his salary to external forces: "My boss gave me that raise probably because he is a nice person. I really don't see how my performance justifies his actions."

On the other hand, a person operating from an internal locus of control would react to the same situation by taking responsibility for the outcome: "That is so nice of my boss to recognize all of my contributions and hard work." In the first scenario, the locus is based on negative perception, where the recipient of a salary increase still feels like a victim, despite the good thing that has happened to him. In the case of the latter, it was a win-win situation where the recipient took responsibility for deserving the pay increase, but he also showed appreciation for his or her boss. Regardless of which locus you operate from, like your perspective, you have shaped it over the course of your life, and your locus of control is really the locus of your perception.

It would be fair to say that during the course of our lives, all of us receive requests from others. However, when necessary, some of us are better able to say "no" to these requests. For different reasons in which we have covered, some have learned effective ways of saying "no" to others and situations that arise. Perhaps it was a combination of positive opportunities provided by the environment of some individuals and their genetic makeup, that contributed to the development of their positive relational skills. Others have made the decision to change what was not working for them and have learned to develop the interpersonal boundaries skills and habits that promote well being.

Regardless if you tend to mostly operate from an external locus, you can change your source of operational power. You can do this by taking responsibility for the choices you make, and when you realize these choices failed work to for you, you can change the way you behave.

6

The Concepts of Self and Selflessness and Boundaries

At birth, we are naturally selfish, believing the world revolves around us. Being fed and feeling warm and safe are all that really matters to infants. During our first year of life, we are one hundred percent dependent on the care of our primary caregiver(s). We become better equipped with the capacity to learn how to share with others as we pass our infancy stage of development. More or less around our toddler stage forward, caregivers play a key role in modeling appropriate selfless behaviors for the child. Parental guidance here assists the child to develop awareness of the needs of others, and we learn that other people matter. Parents do this by teaching children to share their toys or food with others: "Share the ball with Ben" or "Share a cookie with Mary." Children will then reach certain developmental marks where their capacity to regard others becomes more complex. With the proper parental guidance, the child's selfless capacity can expand and self-sustain into his future social.

Selflessness refers to having lower concern for oneself. It is the opposite of being selfish. To be completely selfless one hundred percent of the time is not possible. We require at least a minimal level of self-attention in order to survive, such as attending to our basic needs, such as grooming, and eating, to name a few. Anytime you turn attention to your own needs, you become self-focused, thus not self*less*. In general, some people tend to prioritize engaging in more selfless or altruistic acts than others.

The concepts of self and selflessness are also culturally based. Some societies are more oriented toward the group than the self, in that individuals learn to place greater value on groups, rather than on the individual. Therefore, individuality is generally discouraged in these societies. In the United States, greater value is placed on the individual. Typically, we are encouraged to develop our individuality first.

Nevertheless, for the most part regardless of your culture, people have the need to belong, which motivates our need to care for others. However, relational success requires a healthy balance between the individual and his relationships. When this balance is practiced, giving comes from a genuine place of wanting and not as a learned social mechanism of survival used to prevent negative reactions from others.

We benefit from a balance between the development of individuality and the ability to form healthy relationships to happen naturally in the person's primary environment.

However, as children we rely on key figures in our home environment to guide us to think of others.[1, 2, 19] We learn both selflessness and selfishness at home. Of course, it does not necessarily mean that our parents are selfish, and they failed at teaching selfless behaviors to us. Often, parents lack the ability to be proactive in this regard, such as acting on opportunities for teachable moments that can serve as opportunities to teach children selflessness.

The concept of selflessness is not entirely concrete, which makes it more difficult to fully wrap you head around it. Regardless, as children we do most of our learning through observations and the meaning we assigned to our experiences, and this is what influences the degree of our capacity to balance between selflessness or selfishness.

Throughout our lives, we are consistently challenged with the need to balance the "self" and selflessness. In other words, we are in constant need to protect our sense of self and our self-worth against our need to belong to others or to a group. This takes place in our attempts to form and maintain healthy relationships with others, while simultaneously preserving (often subconsciously) a sense of self, though often feeling that we have failed at this task miserably.[34, 60, 62]

BONDING, IDENTITY AND BOUNDARIES

Social bonds fulfill a basic human need to belong. For this reason, we place great value on how we relate to others. With the high appraisal that we place on our relationships, feeling rejected or rejecting others places a perceived risk on our bonds with others. Human social bonding begins with the primary caregiver, who also assists in facilitating social bonding with other people.[11, 31, 18, 19] The individual is a part of her family system,[19, 94] and people in the family system are driven by two opposing life forces, involving balancing togetherness and individuality—in other words, balancing the "I" with the "we."[74, 82] Togetherness requires a person to develop qualities, and adaptive relational mechanisms needed to relate with others and to sustain these relationships, which is facilitated by our early positive relationships with our caregivers.

Individuality is our ability to develop and sustain our core identity.[97, 101] Thus, the idea is to adequately develop and maintain the two. This concept also involves balancing the self and selflessness, which was just previously discussed. Balancing your individuality in the context of your relationships requires being comfortable with balancing self and selflessness. For instance, the self does not need to suffer in the name of selflessness.

Ideally, we want to be able to balance these two forces, your needs and the needs of the other person (The "I" and the "we"). [60, 74, 82, 118]

Furthermore, being able to balance these two opposing forces (The "I" and the "we) promotes emotional maturity and the differentiation of self within the system of family, which is later transferred into our future relationships in the way we relate to all others we cross paths with (romantic partners, bosses, neighbors, teachers, etc).

A healthy, developed self is implicated in both, the interpersonal and intrapersonal aspects of the person, in which case a person develops the mechanisms needed to have a healthy relationship with herself and others. Again, when this balance is achieved, the "I" does not need to suffer at the cost of the "we," or vice versa.

A well-developed sense of self is prone to be part of more functional, or healthier, interpersonal relationships, because a person with a well-developed self is better able to operate from a more logical, and objective perspective in the context of relationships.[97, 100] The person with a well-developed self is less likely of being easily emotionally reactive to external stimulations, or less likely to operate from an external locus of control.

On the other hand, individuals whose early environments were not optimal in providing opportunities for healthy development, are likely to struggle in their attempt to balance their identity and the needs of their relationships. These individuals also typically have a general negative perception of how others interact with them. They tend to be excessively sensitive and tend to easily and negatively react to the comments or actions of other people. This is because these individuals may be perceiving themselves as being under attack, victimized, or scorned.

On the other hand, the person with an identity that is well developed is less anxious about himself and his interpersonal relationships. Remember, these relational patterns are likely to have been established early in the person's initial interactions within his family system and continued to be shaped over time across the person's stages of development as a result of the new relationships that he ends up having.

MORE ON "WHEN THINGS GO WRONG IN DEVELOPMENT"

When a family system exists within a dysfunctional environment where anxiety makes up the foundation of that relational system, anxiety is what thrives within the environment. The individual learns to be more reactive. So, the individual develops these internal mechanisms that cause the person to be more relationally unstable. These individuals tend to be hypervigilant and fearful in relationships.

These relational anxieties develop from environments that are too unpredictable and do not feel safe, because at one moment the person was maybe expecting to receive love and attention, and the next, instead, she is excessively punished, yelled at, harshly criticized, embarrassed, or left alone.[101, 102, 105] These, of course, are extreme examples. Sometimes, our caregivers had the best of intentions, and yet we still experienced these negative feelings resulting from some sort of an unstable or unpleasant experience.

We all have had experiences in early development that have caused us to feel uneasy. Of course, the intensity of an experience (i.e., how bad it is) impacts how we are shaped. However, frequency and consistency are serious problems: how frequently and how consistently did we experience anxiety from the instability or unpredictability of our early relationships with key figures? Each time you are introduced to these experiences, you become anxious.

Therefore, it is based on the regularity of these inconsistencies and anxieties that you become programmed to respond to such an environment. This is how you learn to socially survive in the world. You gradually learn that your world is unpredictable and your world is scary, as opposed to a person raised in a better-functioning environment, one prone to safety. Someone raised in that type of environment learns trust and dependability, because someone cannot feel safe and scared simultaneously.

Therefore, your brain is going to react in ways that will match that feeling of safety, and your brain wires itself according to the environment. When a person adapts to an environment that is more predictable, safe, and nurturing, the person is programmed to expect and to trust this feeling of safety. The person is less likely to doubt, or to be on edge about their relationships, fearing what is going to happen next. "Am I going to be safe?"

That happens with us. We do this in order to survive. If you put any of us in the middle of a jungle, with or without a weapon even, and we are thrown in the middle of this jungle without skills to survive in the wilderness, we will activate mechanisms within our system to stay alert in order to attempt protect ourselves., such as the fight-or-flight response, discussed earlier in chapter 1. As we have shown, this is a healthy mechanism for our survival which becomes activated in response to perceived threat.

The same mechanism is activated in social situations when we perceive a social threat (e.g., rejection, abandonment). As we have discussed, our brains cannot distinguish between a real threat to our survival, such as being attacked by a wild animal from fear of public speaking, or a social rejection, and responds in the same manner to all those situations alike. This is because of how you have learned to interpret these situations, what they mean to you.

Frequently, saying "yes" against our desire is a subconscious attempt to avoid a potential threat of being rejected or disapproved by others, which again functions as a perceived threat to our (social) survival. We are motivated by our need to belong, to seek bonding and relationships, which includes gaining the approval of others. So, the idea of breaking a bond, or losing a relationship causes fear, and fear motivates people to avoid what they fear. Violation of personal boundaries is an attempt to avoid what we fear. Saying "yes" when you mean "no" avoids disapproval of others; by controlling that, you are taming what you fear. This concept is well illustrated in the case of Carol.

THE CASE OF CAROL

Carol is a twenty-nine-year-old woman who had her "aha!" moment in one of our sessions. After several, as she put it, "failed relationships with the wrong guys," Carol came to the realization that in all of these relationships, she would lose her sense of self in the midst of her anxiety. She noted always trying so hard to accommodate the current partner and his lifestyle. Even her own personal style would drastically change shortly into the early stages of her relationships. She would alter her style of dressing, hair, and even behaviors.

She added that in order to impress her partner, she would pick up a new hobby and drop another, according to how she thought it would please him. Carol also noted that these men had not shown interest in doing things with her. The typical scenario she would settle for would be to watch a movie, order take out, and have sex during the weekdays, as these men always seemed busy on weekends. Carol further disclosed that she never felt secure with any of her previous partners. She would always be so preoccupied with what they were thinking of her that she would forget herself completely.

Carol came from a family of good parents who provided a comfortable life for her. However, her father was a workaholic who she barely knew because he was hardly available to her. Even when he was home, he would be in his home office, and it was common knowledge that she shouldn't interrupt him, because he would become quite angry. Overall, Carol's father was emotionally distant, as was her mother most of time, unless she was in the mood for affection.

Perhaps it was her father's emotional distance and the emotional unpredictability of her mother that created Carol's anxious ways. This all affected how she related to others and was the basis for her intrinsic motivations to please the man in her life, so that he would love her unconditionally. In doing this, she would lose her own sense of self and relate anxiously with these men.

THEORY OF SECURE VS. INSECURE ATTACHMENTS, AND PLEASERS

The style in which we relate with others today has developed early in our relationships with primary caregivers. This concept of early attachment was well explored in the past by pioneers such as psychologists John Bowlby and Mary Ainsworth, and later by Cindy Hazan and Philip Shaver, who have applied attachment theory to adult relationships. Theories of attachment explain certain distinct characteristics in the pattern of which human infants attach to their caregiver, and how this early style of bonding sets the foundation for other relationships over the course of the individual life span.[11, 40, 69, 94]

According to this concept, the capacity for human attachment is instinctive in nature. However, it occurs during a critical period of development, while it is impacted by the interaction of the individual's environment. The learning that takes place during this time will influence adult behavior. Therefore, the style of relationships we end up having with our caregivers is believed to shape the attachment style we will end up having in our future relationships into adulthood.

The adult attachment styles are secure attachment, anxious-preoccupied, dismissive-avoidant, and fearful-avoidant attachment. Actually, these attachment styles can be used to explain aspects of all types of the individuals' relationships, including romantic and sexual relationships, how the person will come to respond to the needs of his or her own children, and a person's relationship with an older adult parental figure, to name a few. A person's attachment style describes the manner, which the person relates, interpersonally and intrapersonally. Over time, the style which a person tends to relate becomes part of fabric of that individual's personality.

The securely attached person finds approaching relationships easy. The anxious-preoccupied person struggles to trust that others love him (*I want to be with her; what if she doesn't what to be with me?*). The dismissive-avoidant person shuts down emotionally to others when he or she feels he or she is getting too close (*I'd rather not get involved; I don't want to depend on others and have others depend on me*). The fearful-avoidant person fears he or she will be hurt when getting close to others (*I want to date her, but what if I get hurt?*).

Attachment styles provide a guide to which can be used to conceptualize our own attachment style. That is, how individually you tend to relate for the most part. Attachment styles play a role in how we go about getting our social needs met, because it is involved in the types of social survival mechanisms we end up developing from our early relationships. For instance, a securely attached person most likely was consistently provided with opportunities to feel secure in his relationship with his caregiver. For example, as a child this individual learned to see his parent as a secure base from which he can independently explore his environment. As a result, of this predictability and reliability offered by his parent or his environment, this individual has learned adaptive mechanism of survival he applies to himself and in his relationships with others. This individual grows up equipped to have similar relationships with others (i.e., stable), such as with romantic partners.

The dynamics in relationships of securely attached individuals are founded on interdependence, and they involve honesty in communicating wants and needs clearly to each other, while boundaries are clearly stated. These relationships involve feeling secure and connected while allowing for the partner to preserve his autonomy and freedom to explore his world independently. The securely attached person is better able to balance individuality and togetherness. This person tends to experience more satisfaction in his or her relationships.

On the other hand, unlike securely attached individuals, relationships of insecurely attached individuals are based on anxiety, preoccupation, and mistrust. These individuals lack autonomy as a result of having consistently experienced insecurities in the relationship with their childhood caregivers. They tend to become emotionally enmeshed with others. As such, they tend to do a poor job at balancing their individuality with their relationships. They use their significant others as a primary base of their fulfilment.

These individuals' insecurities can make them possessive and clingy, which tends to drive other people away. Typically, these individuals do not do well with the independence or autonomy of their partners. For example, individuals with such an insecure attachment style, tend to perceive their partner's pursuit of hobby or friendships as a threat to their own safety in the relationship, such that they might feel unloved and abandoned. This dependence and/or insecurity in relationships causes dysfunctions which reinforces the maladaptive mechanisms of the person, such as those involving low self-worth and trust (*I was right—why would she want to be with me? I knew I couldn't trust anyone!*). Boundaries tend to be unclear among insecurely attached individuals.

As it has been evident in the discussion, people who were not securely attached are likely to develop maladaptive social survival mechanisms in order to cope with their relational anxieties. Triangulation is one of them. This term refers to when a person brings a third element into the dynamics of their dyadic relationship, such as a third person (as in an extramarital affair), a behavior (chronically consuming pornography in place of sexual intimacy with the romantic partner), or substance abuse. Therefore, these become alternate ways a person adapts to survive the stressors in his life.

These coping mechanisms (maladaptive) serve to soothe the person, as a consequence of the missing parts of the "self" that were not fully developed during the first few years of life. They also represent the person's internal working model for relating to oneself and others as they become transferred into a person's future relationships.

It is within the dynamic of individual biological propensities to bond with another person, and in his environment that person's unique style of attachment develops and becomes the foundation for the individual's relational working model [97]. In other words, the individual relational style becomes the blueprint for how each person will relate to and/or form bonds with others throughout his or her life.

There are many different causes that can impact a child in becoming securely attached. Often, the reasons are not intentional and involve circumstances outside of parental control. These include:

- separation from the primary caregiver due to illness, death, and/or adoption

- inconsistencies of the primary caregiver, such as a succession of nannies or staff at a daycare center
- frequent changes of the child's primary immediate environment, such as the case of children in foster care
- lack of adequate parenting skills
- maternal responsiveness reduced by mind-altering substances like alcohol or drugs, or due to maternal depression

THE BRAIN AND ATTACHMENT

Studies, involving placing participants under the FMRI (functional magnetic resonance imaging) machine, related to behavioral responses to rejection and social conflicts, have observed that anxious attachment styles have been associated with more intense behavioral responses to rejections and social conflicts. Studies have also shown that anxious attachments are associated with greater negative emotions, somatic symptoms, and lower self-esteem in response to imagined rejection. Moreover, studies reveal that when individuals were presented with angry faces, associated with negative feedback, individuals higher in attachment anxiety displayed greater activity in their amygdala (again, an affective neuro-region responsible for processing perceived threatening cues, including facial expressions of others).[30, 55, 135, 137]

Therefore, attachment experiences can be implicated in shaping a person's internal blueprint of relationships. As social beings, we develop coping skills in our attempt to keep our social bonds. Initially the parent is expected to meet all of his or her child's basic needs, including food, shelter, love, and support, and to scaffold the child's learning until he or she can attain greater independence. However, consistently insecure relational experiences with our primary caregivers elicit anxiety because they are not a part of the natural process.

BOUNDARY ISSUES AND ATTACHMENT PROBLEMS

Individuals who were anxiously attached as young children experience an undifferentiated sense of self, which means that their identities do not develop properly, such as promoting of individual autonomy. Instead, their identity is likely to become fused or enmeshed with that of key attachment figures in early development. Again, this happens as a result of limited opportunities for positive early relationships, which impacts the development of his identity.

The person's underdeveloped identity and his irrational scripts (such as "*I am not worthy*") lead the development of compensatory mechanisms (used by the person to compensate for his or her perceived flaws). When activated by similar social situations or emotions, these mechanisms are used in the person's attempt to adapt to (or survive) the situation. These mechanisms develop in early stages of life and are activated throughout the course of the person's life. They transfer onto current and future relationships with other people. For example, the individual has a tendency to be more reactive to the emotions of others because an interaction triggers subconscious memories, and along with those memories, associated feelings and emotions are also triggered. Thus, he or she becomes reactive, or fused with the emotions of the other, which is the opposite of being present.

Insecure attachment styles typically involve poor boundaries. This is because the individuals who attach in this manner have learned maladaptive mechanisms of relationship survival in order to deal with their relational anxieties. So, saying "yes" when you mean "no" is your subconscious attempt to control the reaction of others, so that others will not disapprove of you.

Becoming more present in your relationships by asking for clarification from the other person ("What do you mean?") instead of assuming what you perceive is true, helps improve the way you relate with others.

THE DEVELOPMENT OF PLEASING AS A COPING MECHANISMS FOR SOCIAL SURVIVAL

When a child has been exposed to early dysfunctional interpersonal experiences, the child learns early on to compensate for the inadequacies of his environment, and intuitively he or she develops coping mechanisms of survival. For example, those involving a controlling parent (no matter what the child did, it was never good enough to make his or her caregiver happy) or experiences of violence. These mechanisms (frequently, not adaptive) help the child cope with the dynamics of his environment, such as with his relationship with his caregiver. The child learns other relational-compensating mechanisms, which are not adaptive to the development of his social competence. These mechanisms might involve emotional withdrawal in that the child withdraws and eventually isolates himself from others. For example, perhaps when expressing his feelings, the child received excessive criticisms or punishments. In other cases, the child may have had to become *parentified* early on [141]. (This means that the child reversed roles with an immature caregiver and became the one obliged to take care of his caregiver, providing nurturing, attention, and concern for the adult, rather than receiving the care).

Children in these examples intuitively use these social strategies as a way to psychologically adjust to their individual emotions in response to the specific stress of their environment, caused by inappropriate feedback from their caregivers. These early learned experiences of taking care of an adult, or of taking care of another sibling in the place of the adult, tend to lead to adult behaviors consistent with caretaking, or the inability to set effective boundaries with others. When children are placed into a role of an adult they tend to learn that the love they will receive is conditional to their performance of care taking or pleasing the adult whose care they were assigned to, rather than learning that they are loved for who they are.

UNCONDITIONAL VERSUS CONDITIONAL LOVE AND PLEASING BEHAVIORS

Being able to securely attach to our caregivers, and having our needs met provides us with safety and a sense of belonging. These early experiences also allow for emotional regulation in order for the person to be better equipped to connect to and bond with others. It is in how we are loved that we learn how to love others. The more unconditional the love we receive as children, the better we learn to feel about ourselves because the unconditional love we received programmed us to feel good enough to be loved by others no matter what we do, and despite the mistakes we make. So, when this is the case, a person is likely to develop adaptive social competence. Less socially adaptive skills such as pathological pleasing, and or other survival mechanisms tend to not develop.

The more conditions that are placed on the love that we receive from these early experiences, the more likely we are to learn that the love we will receive from other relationships is conditional. So, again, we learn these conditions very early on when our needs for proximity and reassurance that we are loved, no matter what, are discouraged by our caregivers, and we experience insecurities as a result of the emotional absence of our caregiver. Since human beings are highly adaptable, we turn to other coping strategies, such as pleasing, to help us deal with the insecurities that we experience when the forming of these attachment bonds become interrupted or compromised.

As we have discussed, unfortunately, these social coping mechanisms or strategies are not always adaptive to our well-being. For instance, some of us learn to suppress our emotions as an attempt to deal with parental figures who were emotionally unavailable. Maybe we learn to please and please and please as an attempt to make our unhappy parents happier, but we failed to do so because their unhappiness, although at times blamed on us, was not related to us.

It is important to remember that our parents may simply have been repeating the relational styles they have learned from their own parents. Unless a person becomes aware of these dysfunctional interpersonal habits, change and improvement are unlikely to occur. So, it is likely that, like our parents, we, up until the point of reading this book, were not aware of these problems and have been passing down these dysfunctional patterns onto other generations.

Regardless of what your current relationship style is, you are not doomed to it. You can change it. You can learn and adopt new behaviors consistent with the types of relationships you desire having. Tweaking your current behaviors a bit, will help improve the way you relate with others. This is accomplished by gaining awareness about your own relational-behavior patterns and replacing them with new and more effective behaviors.

REFLECTIVE JOURNAL EXERCISE 1

Now take a moment to reflect on the types of relationships you've had and the types of boundary strategies you have used in these relationships.

- How are these relationships similar, and how are they different in the manner in which you established boundaries?
- Have you noticed any changes in the patterns, comparing these relationships over time?
- Which specific behaviors that you identified in your reflections would you like to change?

Take your time to write down your answers. You can do this over several days, if needed.

Overall, take any child with adequate biological predisposition to form healthy relationships, and place him or her into an environment where predictability is lacking, and he or she will be likely to develop patterns of internal responses consistent with the nature of his environment (e.g., hypervigilance, fear). For instance, oftentimes the child may learn that suppressing his or her own feelings is really the best way to survive. Then the child will not express feelings, will remain quieter, and will isolate. Whatever the environment calls for is what the child adapts to in order to survive in that environment.

The inadequacies of the environment will shape the blueprint of a person's relational style, and serve as the foundation for the person's relationships. You are then going to walk into a new relationship with those mechanisms in place. That is all you know. It is how you know how to love and relate to other people. You will be suspicious. You will be reactive. You will attack, feel attacked, feel criticized, or you will flee the area when you are feeling potentially or easily ambushed.

You become used to certain types of environments. Where you learned to be treated by others and to treat others in certain ways is the "normal." You adapted to the familiar environment. Whatever it is that you learned, the message that you took from your years of practice and relational development, will be carried with you into your future relationships. It will shape your perception and guide your behaviors.

Furthermore, you will tap into your internal survival mechanisms (e.g., suspicion) any time you are presented with a situation eliciting similar unsettling feelings and unpredictability of situations from your earlier experiences. Of course, it's not this black and white because at birth we are biologically equipped with different degrees of resilience and predispositions to personality traits, and these too get to interact with the environment (i.e., nature and nurture). So, it is important to consider how the result of this interaction is unique to each individual. For instance, there are some cases which issues of inadequate boundaries and/or pleasing can be severe, as in the case of co-dependence. These cases are not within the scope of this book but it is important that we touch on the topic.

REFLECTIVE JOURNAL EXERCISE 2

It is important to focus introspectively on the types of relationships you had growing up, or what type of relational experience you had with your parents.

- How did your parents love you? Were you encouraged to express your feelings?
- Were you encouraged to try new experiences without fearing mistakes because mistakes would not be taken well by your caregiver? When you made mistakes, were you supported and understood?
- How similar and different are your current relationships compared with your earlier ones?
- Do you remember "breaking your back" to make someone happy? Did it work? Were you appreciated?

7

Types of Pleasers

Throughout this next section, I will discuss the concept of different relational problems because I think it would be helpful in your understanding of the concept of boundaries to learn about its more pathological forms.

We will explore a variety of types of pleasers falling toward the one extreme end of a hypothetical continuum. These include: the codependent, the caretaker, the pleaser, the sociotropic, the octopus pleaser, and the ambivalent pleaser, (the latter of which I have categorized and named in my work in private practice). These are essentially variations of the same thing, that is, sub-categorizations of codependency. Since no one person is alike, these sub-categories seem to provide a more specific description of variations in behavioral pattern clusters, observed among individuals presenting with persistent codependent characteristics. Therefore, for the purpose of this book, let us say that some people may have some codependent tendencies, and others may be more extreme, thus are more fully codependent. However, pleasing is a characteristic of codependency.

The different types of pleasers presented here all represent variations of people's maladaptive relational patterns involving violation of self-boundaries. What they all have in common is that they result from fusing one's own identity with another person. This is because these individuals' development entailed learning and practicing focus attention on the needs of another at the cost of losing their own individuality, practicing excessive self-sacrifice, and self-violation of boundaries.

CODEPENDENCY

For the purposes of this book, I will consider codependency as the extreme form of people pleasing, thus falling in the extreme end of the continuum of higher violation of boundaries. I am providing you with an elaboration upon this concept because I think that the information about codependency can be useful in the understanding of how boundary issues develop, to a large extent, as an environmental byproduct.

The concept of codependency originally evolved from the field of chemical dependency, which originated in the late 1970s, and referred to the relationship dynamics of families of alcoholics in treatment. It was noted that these individuals presented distinct patterns of behavior that attracted the attention of professionals in the chemical-dependency field. These behaviors and attitudes included a pattern of painful dependence on compulsive behaviors and on approval from others, in an attempt to find safety, self-worth, and identity.[128]

Later the meaning of the term codependency, once limited to family members of alcoholics, was expanded to describe people who grew up in dysfunctional families, regardless of the presence of substance abuse. These family members are prone to developing codependency because it is not the substance, per say, that automatically causes a person to become codependent, but the circumstances within the environment.

Parents who are regular users of substances are unable to be emotionally attuned with their offspring, whose own emotional regulation is dependent on their caregivers. Therefore, home environments where a key authority figure is under the influence of a substance, or who is making regular use of a substance, are an environment prone to dysfunctional relationships with offspring and others in his proximity. This dysfunctional disconnection resulting from the use of substances is what leads to the development of codependency among family members.[101, 127, 140]

Codependency can be defined as external focusing, self-sacrificing, controlling of others, and suppressing one's own emotions. (These defining features were drawn from a variety of published definitions of codependency.) Another distinct feature of codependency is poor interpersonal boundaries.[34] Furthermore, the literature suggests that codependency stems from the development of survival behaviors that evolve in dysfunctional families, where children learn to overcompensate for the inadequacies of their primary caregivers and their immediate environment (i.e., home), and come to develop an excessive sensitivity to the needs of others.

It has been proposed by some, that codependency is a disease involving the loss of self-hood,[105] fundamentally leading to a distorted relationship with self and others. In other words, codependents tend to neglect their own needs and develop other-oriented caretaking behaviors as an attempt to seek self-identity and emotional fulfillment through these external relationships.

Therefore, codependency is marked by other-oriented caretaking patterns, which are excessive and occur at the cost of a person's well-being as an attempt to maintain and secure relationships. Furthermore, codependency not only includes an underdeveloped sense of self, but it also includes boundary distortions, which pose challenges in relationships. Codependency symptoms can also be correlated with early development involving perfectionistic, authoritarian, inadequate or dysfunctional home environments. Home environments consisting of emotionally or physically absent parents is also correlated with the development of codependency.

These environments have forced the person to adapt accordingly. That is, the individual, in his or her best attempt to socially survive his environment, developed a set of behavioral traits.

On the other hand, some studies have indicated that codependency is a universal human condition, rather than a culturally specific element. Codependency involves the emotional support of others, while at the same time it can involve feelings of anxiety and ambivalence, resulting from this excessive care.[141] Therefore, codependency is a learned behavior, which is reinforced by a person's social systems and values, and the ongoing opportunities to relate with others in the world. Persons who fit this profile are not necessarily aware of their codependent thinking patterns and behaviors. This is because these behaviors and thinking patterns are mechanisms the person has developed to deal with his or her environment, which evolved over time, and the person has practiced these mechanisms ever since. Therefore, these features have become subconscious, so tend to occur automatically, or as the person's "second nature."

THE CARETAKER

Caretaking is a feature of codependency. However, it is frequently used as a stand-alone individual characteristic. The caretaker seeks to make others in his or her environment (who are capable of doing for themselves) his or her big babies. This dynamic is inappropriate and dysfunctional, as discussed earlier, unless this level of care is provided to young children or an ill or unable person. The caretaker anticipates the needs of others and is involved in everything as an attempt to fix and do for others, as if they cannot do for themselves. The caretaker expects to receive the recognition that others cannot live without him or her. Threats to this dysfunctional relationship are in realizing that an individual can actually live without the caretaker. This can cause a great deal of distress and fatigue for the caretaker.

THE PLEASER

"Pleaser" is another unofficial label used to describe individuals who, at the cost of their own well-being, consistently place the happiness of other people before their own. Like the caretaker and the codependent, the pleaser has learned to control the reactions of others by saying "yes," bending over backward to please at the cost of his or her own well-being. The focus of otherness here is ensuring that others do not become upset with you. So, you suppress your own needs by saying "yes" when you mean "no," or you simply stay quiet about your dislikes in order to avoid upsetting others. You exercise great control over others by ensuring you are always liked. Threats to this dysfunctional relationship are at the realization that an individual can actually still be disappointed with you over the thought you sacrifice so much of yourself to please. This can cause a great deal of distress and fatigue for the person.

In one study, social pressure relating to eating was assessed in 101 college students who were asked to complete a questionnaire assessing characteristics for people pleasing, also known as "sociotropy."[225] Findings indicated that students with higher scores on the scale of "people pleasing" were more likely to give-in to the pressure of accepting eating the candies that were handed to them, even when it was against their will to eat them. Findings also revealed that people pleasers in the study reported their motivation for accepting the candies was an attempt to make the other person feel more comfortable [43].

Often, the receiver can thrive on receiving, or on being cared for. However, this also causes tension, depending on the types of expectations of his or her giver. Don't get me wrong, it is okay to formulate expectations about others, as long as these expectations are realistic for the other person. Unfortunately, having unrealistic expectations of others, including those in close proximity to us, is prevalent in dysfunctional relationships involving codependents and/or pleasers. In other words, the pleaser would "break his back" for his partner, who might also be dysfunctional in their own way, so have limited capacity to appreciate the pleaser. This type of dynamic involving partners who fit the profile of chronic pleasers tends to be typical in "codependent" dysfunctional relationships. In fact, it is this combination that sustains the dysfunctionality.

THE OCTOPUS PLEASER

This is a term I came up with to sub-classify individuals with certain pleasing patterns. Specifically, pleasers with the "Octopus" trait attempt to do everything they can to get their "tentacles" on a situation. This is an attempt to insure increased recognition and appreciation from others. The Octopus works hard at doing "all" the work, and doing it "perfectly," in order to make others happy. However, over time the Octopus becomes tired, anxious, and even angry, because everyone seems to look for the octopus to get the job done and no one seems to appreciate the hard work and the perfection, the skillful multitasker "I got this!" Octopus does. Like codependents and people pleasers, the happiness of the Octopus pleaser is dependent on the happiness of others. Also, this person is not "dependent" on other people in the general sense of the word, but emotionally he or she is. It is this emotional dependency on the happiness and satisfaction of other people that motivates the pleasing behaviors of pleasers and codependents alike, which comes from the tendency for pleasers to be other-focused rather than self-focused.

In my observations, people with the octopus pleasing traits specifically seem to have been raised in an environment demanding perfectionism, where these people experienced their efforts as never being enough, resulting in a need to strive for more perfection. Also, being a child in a home where the primary caregiver was physically or mentally ill, resulting in the child to experience consistent lack of control, is another common pattern I have identified in the upbringing of people with the octopus behavioral trait.

THE AMBIVALENT PLEASER

This term refers to persons are conflicted in that they tend to isolate themselves from others, while at the same time they need and seek approval from others. The ambivalent pleaser does not allow others to get too close. These individuals tend to slip away at the possibility of becoming a part of something, so as to avoid letting others know them well. This may be because they are too afraid to reveal their perceived "inadequate" true self. The focus of "otherness" here is to please others in order to sustain their positive view of the pleaser. The ambivalent pleaser usually accomplishes this by staying in relationships just long enough before others get to know the "real me,", or the pleasers perceived inadequacies. Often, this individual leaves the relationship or before she experiences the outcome of her commitment. She accomplishes this by not committing to long-term relationships, jobs, or any other such endeavor. Herr short stay in the lives of other people, or in the context of commitments, also ensures that others do not become disappointed with her.

If you are an ambivalent pleaser, you also learn to suppress your own needs by saying "yes" when you mean "no," or simply to stay quiet about your dislikes in order to avoid upsetting others. You exercise great control of others by ensuring you are always liked. Threats to this dysfunctional relationship are any realization that an individual can actually still be disappointed with you even though you sacrificed so much of yourself to please him or her. This can cause a great deal of distress and fatigue for the ambivalent pleaser.

While a person's tendency to be more other-focused is thought to develop over the course of life, at times this can evolve later. For instance, certain relationships that come about later in our lives help establish in us a tendency to please. This might be excessive in comparison to our typical way. For example, some of us might have behaved completely out of character toward one person in our lives, such as a girlfriend or boyfriend, and we don't know why. This is because of what each unique relationship dynamic elicits in those involved. In other words, the combination of partners and the internal pre-dispositions of each one give birth to a new whole unique to that combination of beings. So, that is why every relationship is unique.

The above pleasing and codependent categories share core similarities involving overall extreme other-focused and self-sacrificing tendencies. In fact, they consistently overlap in their characteristics and in how they are likely to have developed. Again, generally speaking, being a caretaker or a pleaser of any type are features of codependency per its definitions provided earlier in this chapter. However, I am not attempting to diagnose you as codependent if you identify yourself as one who generally pleases others. In reality, we all do please from time-to-time. What we are looking for is where we stand in the continuum of healthy/functional to dysfunctional, what this means in our relationships with others, and once this awareness has been raised, choosing to do something about it. The goal is to improve our ability to maintain individual autonomy within a relationship.

In other words, it is crucial for our personal and social well-being to improve our ability to maintain and protect our individual identity, personal goals, and needs while attending appropriately to our relationships or interactions with others, in general.

It is important to note that, although pleasers are always doing for others, their underlying and mostly subconscious motivation of self-sacrifice is for self-fulfillment, which does not promote mutual benefits for anyone involved. In general, codependent, caretaking, and pleasing relationships are comprised of a sense of perceived control, where the codependent caretaker, or pleaser, pleases in order to conform with the majority, to gain love, acceptance, and a sense of purpose on the eyes of others. Since the focus of the pleaser is on others, their giving tends to be motivated from a place of self rather than selflessness. This type of relationship dynamic typically involves unrealistic expectations from those whom the pleaser is pleasing.

Since relationships that involve controlling others do not work, the pleaser becomes easily frustrated and even angry at his failure to control through his sacrifices. The type of person on the receiving end of this type of relationship frequently also lacks the independence required for a successful interdependent relationship. [132] Therefore, based on this concept, the motivation to please comes down to fulfilling the pleaser's own need to please

These other-focused characteristics found among pleasers, caretakers, and codependents do not play well with the concept of interdependence or interdependent relationships. Interdependence will be more fully discussed in chapter 8. However, in general, interdependence is a type of relationship dynamic that involves two or more independent individuals (independent in most aspects) who are able to balance individual autonomy within the context of their relationships.

Interdependence is the opposite of codependency in that it does not involve inappropriate self-sacrifice of one's own needs, violation of boundaries, or lack of reciprocity. Instead, interdependence involves the health of an interpersonal relationship which is dictated by the emotional well-being of the people involved.

Simply put, compared to codependency, interdependence can be illustrated as a two-way street, while codependence involves a one-way street *only!* Interdependence is a cooperative, involving the union of autonomous persons voluntarily meeting their personal and common relational goals. Interdependence does not involve power and control, instead it thrives on democracy and regard among those involved, where reciprocal respect, regard, and compassion for others are practiced.

BREAKING THE HABIT OF DYSFUNCTIONAL RELATIONSHIPS

In order to go from having dysfunctional relationships to healthy ones, we need to change the current attitude about ourselves by getting out of our social comfort zone and behaving in a non-codependent, non-pleasing, and non-caretaking way. We need to continue to be patient with the process and adopt a degree of courage to feel the discomfort associated with the symptoms of fear and anxiety, which are part of the process of change. This will require changing your mindset to goal orientation.

In order to have healthy relationships, we must be healthy. We must adopt the attitude of treating ourselves well, without the cost of others. When you chronically sacrifice yourself for others, you always want something in return, and this is the price others pay. You can set new relational goals, which involves a win-win situation. No one needs to lose for another to win.

Little-by-little you can change your behaviors to align with that of a person of high self-worth. Practice them until they become your new default. Assert your wants and needs by "faking it until you make it," and your emotions will follow. When you begin to establish boundaries with those you fear disapproving of you, you begin to give these individuals a new opportunity to view you from a different perspective. Additionally, in doing so, you will appear more intriguing and attractive to others. Assessing your behaviors in context of your relationships can help you determine the nature of your relationships. Are they functional? o you feel fatigued? Do you feel as though you do not know who you are anymore? Did you get tired of trying to explain or make your point, so now you just stay quiet?

Frequently, people in dysfunctional relationships see their relationships as normal. This is because we tend to think of dysfunctional relationships as those involving physical violence or loud fights. Unfortunately, dysfunctional relationships can also be quiet, leaving you confused and looking for ways to make sense of things and reasons to explain how you feel. You feel depleted and lost, and you don't seem to know why.

There are many different types of dysfunctional relationships that are the result of poor boundary skills. For example, consider a situation involving an individual who has poor interpersonal boundaries. Saying "yes" when he means "no" is his mantra. Others around him call this person the "nice guy" who likes to do things for people. But the nice guy in this story, or the pleaser, feels exhausted and described his situation as "burnout." This is expected because the person who is saying "yes" also has his own commitments in life, and as we have seen, when we say "yes," we are impacting our entire system.

Therefore, by the time the "nice guy" is left to attend to his own work, goals, or anything else that should matter most to him, he becomes compromised by his inability to say "no." This pleaser finds himself in a hamster wheel as he continues to please, in order to prevent disappointing others of their perceived expectation of him as the "nice guy." Unless this person stops saying "no"to himself, his burnout will prevail. This type of dynamic takes place in many types of relationships, and pleasers like the "nice guy" from the example, are likely to behave this way across all settings of their lives (e.g., romantic relationships).

Another reason why people may not realize that their relationship is dysfunctional is because the giver (the one doing all of the sacrifice) and the receiver, are usually not aware of their individual characteristics. This is because their characteristics evolved separately over time and became a part of each individual's relational style. In order for the problem to come to light, each individual would have to develop awareness of the role each plays in the dynamics of their relationship, such as how his or her thoughts and behaviors impact the relationship.

Often times, awareness is attained with the assistance of a professional. For example, this happens when symptoms of the dysfunctional relationship cause one of the partners to seek help for the relationship itself, or for symptoms related to the problems they are having in their relationship. For instance, a pleasing or caretaking partner might seek help when exhausted from the one-way giving and the ongoing disappointment resulted from the unreasonable expectations she has placed on her partner. The same goes for the receiving partner, who can grow overwhelmed by the highly controlling pleaser-partner who gives and gives in a self-sacrificing manner and eventually grows disappointed at her partner for failing to meet her expectations.

It is ok to do things for others, and is an important part of being human. For example, maternal care for young children who are dependent on parental care is appropriate, and as the child grows older, the level and type of care are adjusted accordingly. Also, caring for an older adult in need of care, or an ill person, is also appropriate. However, placing individual needs aside to consistently do for those who can do for themselves is unhealthy. Therefore, I am not saying you should not do nice things for others, such as bringing your partner breakfast in bed sometimes. However, in healthy relationships these types of gestures are reciprocal after all, right?

On the other side of the coin, a functional relationship requires reciprocity and the preservation of each individual's autonomy. This means that we need to maintain our sense of self when giving. The problem often found in unhealthy relationship dynamics where boundaries are lacking is that the predominant motivation and focus of one person is other people.[137, 138]

Persons who we are referring to as "codependent," "people pleasers," and "caretakers," among other terms, is because of their overall more severe other-focus tendencies. These labels also signify the overall relational style of a person. In other words, people who fit these categories for the most part are known to consistently place the needs of others before their own.

These other-focused motivations stem from the need to gain acceptance, validation, appreciation, and love from other people. Therefore, extremely poor interpersonal boundaries, typical among these individuals, are a result of their lack of autonomy and self-preservation.

On a side note, you now know you can improve your ability to establish healthy boundaries with yourself and other people. You also now know that in order to accomplish this, it is helpful to learn the role you play in your interactions with others. For example, what do you communicate with other people when you say "yes" when you mean "no"? This type of introspection (looking inside oneself) promotes an increase in self-awareness, which again is our ability to become a witness of ourselves in our own lives. Self-awareness promotes insights of what we do and why we do the things we do, so then we can attempt to "fix it." In other words, once we know the role we play in our interactions with others, we can change our perception and our behaviors to attain more desirable relational outcomes, which is quite empowering, I think!

- After having read this chapter, I wonder if you can identify yourself with any of the characteristics of a pleaser or a codependent?
- If so, how do you believe this has impacted your life?

It doesn't really matter what type of pleaser you label yourself to be. Rather, it is more important for you to identify the consistent, ineffective pleasing behaviors you have learned and practiced, and begin the process of replacing them with other healthier, boundary-prone behaviors.

REFLECTIVE JOURNAL EXERCISE 2

You have already been asked to answer some of the reflective questions below. However, because you have reached this point in book, I would like for you to answer them again. Compare your answers with those from the first time you answered these questions.

1. In what areas of your life and what aspects of yourself you believe you have the most problems with boundaries (e.g., saying "yes" when you mean "no," remaining silent instead of sharing your opinion, or asking for what you want)?

2. In which of your relationships do you believe you struggle most with boundary problems, for example with romantic partners, parents, or friends?

3. What is it about these relationships that makes it harder for you to set limits?

4. What would you have liked to do differently in these relationships?

    a. Write down your fears related to this situation, such as what stops you from behaving assertively. What do you fear?

    b. What do you think would be the worst thing that could happen if you were to be assertive or do what you fear?

    c. Write down any evidence you have in support of your assumptions being true, such as any proof you might have to support that your fear is true. What would be the outcome of you expressing your needs, or setting your boundaries with the person in your scenario? What do you think the person would think? And how might he or she react?

Part 2

8

Can an Old Dog Learn New Tricks?

The good news is that it is actually possible to "teach an old dog new tricks." Whether our development was adaptive to our wellbeing or not, we are continuously learning and evolving from our experiences. We are born with the necessary mechanisms needed to learn and grow. We have both, an adaptive brain and a body that will adjust to our needs, and learning. Furthermore, learning takes place in both the conscious and the subconscious mind, which means you can either direct your learning, or you can continue to learn without your own direction.

Contributions from science have made it easier to understand how humans learn. It is known that our brain is plastic,[7,134] which means it has the capacity to change (*neuroplasticity*). In other words, the learning and practice of new information and behaviors, lead to the development of corresponding neuro pathways in different brain regions. This capacity of our brains promotes re-adjustment and adaption to accommodate new knowledge and new patterns of thoughts and behaviors.

The concept that our brain has this capacity to reshape itself through learning and practice is not a new idea. The fact that we know about the concept of neuroplasticity is what is new-*sh (within the 20th century)*. In fact, the concept that our brain has the capacity to change in our response to the environment, that is learning and practicing has been well documented. For instance, one well known study discovered that London taxi drivers have a larger hippocampus compared to London bus drivers.[387] The hippocampus is a brain structure involved in long term memory including the storage of past knowledge and experiences, and spatial representations required in learning navigation of the complex routes of London. The study also indicated differences in sizes of the driver's hippocampus to be correlated with the length of time that they were taxi drivers, suggesting that the length of time practicing this task, that is driving, corresponded to changes in brain region in response.

So, just because you have the habit of violating your own boundaries does not mean you need to accept it as your eternal fate since your brain is always changing. The brain is always rewiring (opening new connections or regions) or strengthening existing connections in response to the interaction between our sensory system and our internal (inside body and mind) and external environments (our relationships and physical environment). This happens in an orchestrated fashion, as several brain regions are responsible for one task. The mind is also involved in the process where old information is activated as we try to make sense of the new.

In other words, we naturally attempt to find a point of reference to make sense of new information. This is how we also keep repeating the same ineffective patterns of behavior as we look for prior knowledge or existing patterns of the familiar. If you remember, this principle also explains the concept of perception.

We can direct this ability to change or learn once we have identified what we want to modify (we have acquired awareness). So, if you believe you would like to replace a habit that is not adaptive to your well being, such as habits related to violation of interpersonal boundaries, you can change your behavior to be consistent with healthy boundaries, and you can practice it until it becomes a new habit.

WHAT'S IN IT FOR YOU?

I am going to assume that the reason you are reading this book is because you have identified with the topic to some degree. You probably feel wary of others and situations and have had a hard time saying "no" to them. Or, when you finally say "no," you end up experiencing intense feelings of guilt that make it even harder for you to say "no" the next time around. We both know that guilt is a common denominator among pleasers. So, then you continue to please others from a place of *not* wanting, a place of fear. Thus, in an attempt to control the reactions of others, you say "yes" to please them. Eventually you become resentful of others, and especially of yourself for not saying "no." You may simply be tired of pleasing. Then, you burst out in rage toward those you pleased, or you redirect the anger you feel toward the person your pleased, or yourself for pleasing again, to an unrelated person or situation. Often this happens in ways completely out of the blue or disproportionate to the situation at hand, leaving all those around you puzzled with your exaggerated response. Does this sound familiar?

REFLECTIVE JOURNAL EXERCISE 1

- Think of a time when you were able to replace an old behavioral habit and or thought pattern that was not serving you with a new behavior, or a new way of thinking that has more likely benefited you.
- How did it feel to get yourself out of your comfort zone of the old, that is your old behavior pattern and adjusting to the new, a new way of seeing and doing things?
- What aspect of you/your life would you consider improving but you fear getting out of your comfort zone?

HABITS

We have a brain that matches our habits, including our relationship habits. Habits form through the repetition of behaviors and thoughts. When we learn new information, a behavior, or a thought pattern and we practice it consistently, the "it" that is practiced become automatic, or second nature. It has formed into a new habit.[83]

Habits are a set of behavioral or thought patterns that have been consistently practiced until they have become almost involuntary. A person's daily routines, such as brushing their teeth, daily showers, their diet, and exercise habits consist of a person's established habits. Certain regularly practiced skills, such as the person's ability to operate a vehicle for driving, are learned in the same manner as our habits. Once they are shaped, they occur automatically. They have become second nature to you.

The same goes for our overall disposition to life (e.g., having an optimistic versus a pessimistic outlook of life), which also consists of a habit. We are habituated to view life in a certain way. This is because the way in which we have learned to view our world and relate to it has been practiced over the course for our life. This practice has been made perfect by the way you and I tend to think and behave, again and again, as an optimist, pessimist, or skeptic, to name a few.

Furthermore, habits are such that removing them will naturally cause discomfort. Habits can be good or adaptive to a person's wellbeing, such as having the habit of exercising daily, being generally optimistic, and exercising healthy boundaries. But habits can also be bad or not adaptive, such as in the case of substance addiction, being generally overly pessimistic, and regularly exercising poor boundaries. Pleasing or codependency involves habitually focusing on the wellbeing of others at the cost of your own, which does not consist of an adaptive habit.

Habits help us on the day-to-day by facilitating the accomplishment of certain tasks without us having to think too much about them. Habits are also implicated in the maintenance of our overall well being. For example, we brush our teeth every day to maintain proper hygiene. It also helps us in our social connections because hygiene is important to others as well.

So, we both agree that a daily tooth brushing is an adaptive habit. Now, as you know, brushing your teeth occurs for the most part on automatic pilot. Most of us do not need reminders to brush our teeth because the habit has already been established. In other words, we simply do it at certain times of the day. However, if by any chance we skip brushing, we will most likely miss the feeling we experience afterward. In general, when we break a routine or a habit, we will feel as though we are missing something. That is because breaking a habit or a routine will feel uncomfortable. It places us outside of our comfort zone.

Another characteristic of habits is that since they occur on autopilot, they are actually occurring subconsciously. Sometimes you notice you are brushing your teeth, sometimes you do not; sometimes you see yourself reach for the brush and the toothpaste, and sometimes you do not. This characteristic helps us free up the brain from every possible daily function we have to execute, thus reducing brain overload. The brain can only focus on one task at a time. So, if all of these tasks we do regularly required our undivided focus, we would be on overload and less able to do as much. This is because focus requires brain power and energy that the brain gets to spare during brief rests.

The same occurs with driving. When we first learn to drive, we give our undivided attention to the steps involved in accomplishing the skill of operating the vehicle. Thus, driving at this stage does not feel like second nature because the knowledge is new to the brain and to our motor system involved in this task. Since driving skills in the early stages of learning to drive is still new to the brain, the brain has not yet formed connections in association with this task that would make it feel like second nature to a person. Thus, it has not yet developed into a habit. After we master the skill through repeated practice, our brain will now be programmed (wired) to perform the task without focus; it has become second nature.

Of course, driving does necessitate focusing on the road, and it involves using your best judgment as you pay attention to different things happening on the road every time you drive. We are referring here to our ability to habituate to operating a vehicle for driving. Very much like typing, we do not think of the operation component of typing; instead, we focus on the content we are typing.

Both driving and typing are repetitive skills. It becomes second nature, like brushing our teeth. You do not have to think about how to do it. We have also grown used to the way we interact with ourselves and others. As we discussed earlier and will continue to discuss throughout the remainder of book, we have learned our interpersonal and intrapersonal habits early in our lives from our environment through adaptation, reinforcement, and modeling our caregivers.

Just like brushing our teeth is a good habit, we learn good and bad behavioral habits, such as aggression in dealing with a disagreement versus discussion, or choosing a healthy lifestyle versus not. These conscious or subconscious behavioral habits (good or bad) are practiced throughout our lives, and unless we take notice of those which are not serving us well, we will not be able to change them.

The same thing happens when we learn to play an instrument. We learn and practice it until playing becomes second nature and we can play a difficult instrument like the violin. It also happens with our behavioral habits in the way we behave with ourselves and others. In order to change the way we relate to others, we are required to adopt and practice new ways to relate, and after a while (once our brains have adapted) we will be able to play the violin of our relationships.

CREATURES OF HABIT

We are creatures of habit, and as we have discussed earlier, habits develop over time. As we have also discussed, habits are such that when we change them, this process causes discomfort. Habits constitute internal or external behaviors that are practiced over and over again in a subconscious, compulsory, effortless manner. Habits are adaptive or maladaptive to our well-being, as they do not only include being habituated to depend on a substance, such as drugs and alcohol, or a behavior like gambling or sex addictions.

The nature of a person's pattern of thinking consists of a formed, internal habit. Whether we are overall more pessimistic or optimistic in how we perceive life is a formed habit. We develop habits to think in a certain way, and our thinking patterns or habits establish the default of how we think.

In order for a person who tends to be more pessimistic in how she thinks to change her overall thinking pattern to be optimistic, the person has to relearn a new thinking pattern. This will take effort and practice until it is established as a regular pattern or habit, at which point it will have taken over the old habit or the old way of thinking (the pessimistic way). Unless practiced consistently, these new ways of thinking would not be able to form into new habits because the person will continually revert to the default way of thinking.

Some habits are much more embedded than others because they have evolved and have been established for a longer period of time, maybe even in early development, as we have seen in the case of many people pleasers. It is likely these individuals have learned to think and behave consistent with the meaning they have taken from their early experiences with others. Therefore, internal habitual patterns that have been established early in our development or through our personal life evolution (the way we generally think and are motivated to behave) are not always apparent and are harder to break.

So, again, many of our habits take place on a subconscious level; we are unaware of them. Changing our thinking habits is difficult, but we can change our behaviors such as in the way we choose to interact with other people. Although, this is also difficult it is more easily attainable as long as you are determined to getting out of your comfort zone and take some risks.

This change in behavior will eventually begin to impact how you think. For instance, going from the habit of constantly saying "yes" against your will to becoming better able to establish healthy boundaries will make you feel good. This new feeling will more positively impact your perception, thus making it more a match for how you now behave and feel. The outcome of more positive interactions with others and with yourself, will little by little change your irrational rooted belief system

YOUR BRAIN MATCHES YOUR BEHAVIORS, THOUGHTS, AND FEELINGS

Our feelings match our thoughts. You cannot feel good while having bad thoughts, and vice versa. The types of thoughts you consistently practice, or think, establishes the overall nature of your thought patterns, and consequently, establish how you feel in general.

We have a brain that matches our overall nature of thinking, feeling, and behaving. The same concept applies to our brain's response to our habits, in that we will have a brain that matches our habits. Whether our habits are subconscious or conscious, the brain must re-adjust simultaneously to accommodate new habits as they are forming.[7, 30, 55] Learning occurs in the same manner. Neurons fire together and establish strong connections in response to learning.

Again, let's say you want to learn how to play the piano for the very first time. Your brain has not formed or established the pathway for that skill yet, and that is why it will be difficult at first. It will take learning and practicing. So, you begin to take lessons and practice daily. After a short while, you will find that you can already play a song or two. This is evidence that your brain has begun to accommodate and adapt for that new skill. In other words, neural-connections have evolved to accommodate that skill.

From the early stages of learning the piano, certain neurons began to fire and connect into a cluster or pathway that involves all the elements you need to accomplish the task of playing the piano, and that means your motor-skill development as well (i.e., the fluidity of your fingers). As you continue to practice over time, your brain pathway associated with that skill will only become denser and stronger, so that information will be processed faster. You will be able to respond to music faster, until playing the piano becomes mastered and second nature to you.

The same is true for all that we practice, whether it is internally (thought patterns) or externally (behaviors). You have a brain that matches your current habits, and your current habits match your brain. The brain adapts to what you practice. As a pleaser, your brain has adapted to your pleasing traits and behaviors. However, as we have established, being a pleaser is not adaptive to your wellbeing.

Fortunately, as we have discussed, through the process of learning and practicing, and our brain's capacity to change, we can replace our pleasing habits with other more adaptive ones. Generally speaking, you get to choose how you operate in life. If the way you currently behave feels bad, you can change your behaviors to match the types of feelings you desire to experience. For instance, you can change from habitually saying "yes" out of fear of displeasing another person, to saying "yes" when you actually want and mean it.

HERE'S MORE ON HOW YOU CAN TEACH AN OLD DOG NEW TRICKS

The brain has to develop, or wire itself, in response to new learning because of this capacity, it can also rewire in response to learning new habits that will replace the old ones. So, the idea of changing internal habits is quite promising. Just like with the piano example, you can introduce a new skill, a new way of looking at life and interacting with others. You practice this until your brain has adjusted to the new skill, or until your brain comes to match your new desired self. This will require taking your brain out of its comfort zone in relation to aspects of yourself you want to change.

Remember from earlier discussions that the definition of habits involves the idea that by removing it, will cause discomfort, which means feeling uncomfortable is crucial for the changes to occur. In addition, you will be required to constantly practice the new habit, just like with the example of learning to play the piano. If you do not practice a new thought or behavior consistently, brain pathways for that skill will not strengthen enough for the skill to be mastered. In other words, pathways are formed based on how frequently the knowledge and skill are being reintroduced.[8, 41, 134]

Also remember that you will never be done. You must develop what Carol Dweck calls a mindset of growth in her book, <u>Mindset: The New Psychology of Success</u>. This means you will need to shift focus from being a self-critic, and seeing your challenges as opportunities for growth and change.

You will also be required to always practice newly learned skills, because what you don't use, your brain will lose. Especially when the goal is to replace internal habits, such as people pleasing which likely have evolved from early development. These types of habits are deep rooted, which makes us vulnerable to reverting back to practicing them if we don't stay focused with how we want to behave.

According to one study, the that it takes for creating a new habit can vary depending on the type of habit, and it can take 18 to 254 days to create. [83, 111] To master your new habit requires conscious or subconscious practice. On an average, it is thought that it takes approximately sixty days to form a new habit.[83] You became a people pleaser by developing interpersonal habits to accommodate the trait of pleasing.

You have practiced for a long time this habit of being a people pleaser.

Having been a people pleaser for some time, you are quite skilled at violating your own boundaries, and changing this habit to a more adaptive one will require time and consistent practice, as well. After you introduce a new habit and you begin practicing it, it won't be long until you begin to notice evidence of how your brain is accommodating the new way because you will begin to feel more comfortable with saying no, and you will enjoy the process.

One important thing to keep in mind is that it does not get better if you do not do anything about changing what is not working for you; that is, being a pleaser. In fact, it only gets worse, because the more we practice pleasing others, the more we violate boundaries that protect our well being. Continuing to do that will only cause more frustrations, and even resentment, which again are not positive contributors to our well being. Furthermore, as discussed earlier, the brain's neuro pathways become stronger with practice. When we choose to stay where we are, even if the way we are is not working for us, we are only practicing more of the same, thus strengthening the pathways associated with that which is not working.

FREE WILL VERSUS DETERMINISM, AND BOUNDARY HABIT CHANGE

How much of what happens to us and our interpersonal relationships is really within our control? The way we choose to react to others around us is within our control. We have the free will to choose the direction and the type reaction. However, it is important to develop self-awareness in order to improve your ability to relate with others. The more you learn about yourself the more you can determine how your habitual patterns of behaviors can serve you or hurt you. Once this is accomplished, you can then decide to change the way you react to others. So, your free will is most effective once you have insight. After all, you cannot fix what you do not know is broken.

MORE ON HABIT CHANGE

Getting your brain out of its comfort zone is difficult. The concept speaks for itself. You might feel uncomfortable, stressed, and even scared. This experience of discomfort is your indicator that you are on the right track, and on your way to positive change. The introduction and practice of new behavior requires that your brain begins to wire new pathways in response. Eventually, you will have a brain that better matches the new behaviors, and these new behaviors or thought patterns will become your new default patterns.

But, until this happens, you will feel out of your comfort zone, and this can provoke some degree of stress and fear, which is a normal part of the process. Remember that being in your comfort zone does not mean feeling a "warm and cozy" type of comfort. If the thought of getting out of your comfort zone demotivates you, think for a minute about how you are already living with much anxiety and fear resulting from how you have been doing things, and by perpetuating ineffective thoughts and behaviors.

In other words, you have become accustomed to feeling the fears and anxieties resulting from your perceived lack of control. Again, these fears and anxieties you experience do not feel good, and they get in your way. You learn to desire better results while doing things in the same manner. You live in a never-ending cycle, a hamster in a wheel chasing after more self-esteem and better relationships, while behaving in ways that will only bring you dysfunctional ones.

As you can see, in order to change, you will be required to do things differently, which will cause you to feel anxiety and fear of the unknown and the unfamiliar. You will feel uncomfortable. However, it will be moving you to a destination of an improved self. You will begin to detach from what does not serve you and adopt a new way of thinking and behaving that is consistent with what you want. This idea can be the most challenging when it comes to changing interpersonal habits. However, you want to think of small steps and practice.

It is important to keep in mind that first you need to have realistic expectations of yourself, because changes occur gradually. Change will require you to feel uncomfortable, and again, feeling uncomfortable is your indicator that you are on your way toward change. Second, this process involves having realistic expectations of others, because they will react internally or externally to your changes. In other words, people around you have grown accustomed to the old you. Finally, because you will be a novice at the new behaviors, you are likely to show some inconsistencies, and people might become confused about what to expect of you.

Keep in mind that as creatures of habit, we also habituate others to expect certain behaviors and reactions from us. And, because others are also creatures of their own habits, they will feel discomfort at this new presentation of you. This is a normal process to which, at times, you will be surprised how quickly others will adjust. There will also be times of reaction and resistance, where others might push to see how far they can go before you break. They will test your new boundaries. For instance, others might attempt to manipulate you into guilt or into giving into their request, or might even react by being disappointed and angry at you. However, the choice of living your life more effectively continues to be yours.

In response to negative reactions and barriers that others present, you will have your own barriers as a result of your lack of experience in doing things differently. These include saying "no" to a request from someone who is accustomed to having you accept all requests. Again, you might experience irrational thinking, fears, anxieties, and feelings of guilt associated with the process of learning to reconstruct the old pleasing self as an effective self.

Irrational thinking might overwhelm your mind with obsessions related to how another person now thinks of you: *Will they hate me? Have I done the right thing?* Following these irrational and obsessive thoughts are the feelings the thoughts will evoke, which are not the most desirable types, since our feelings will always match our thoughts. For instance, fear and anxiety are frequently experienced as a result of stepping out of your comfort zone. You begin to feel you have lost your ability of perceived control over the reaction of the other person to whom you would have otherwise said "yes." You also fear the related consequences of this, such as of being rejected, among other things.

When you finally begin to implement healthy boundaries with others, underlying beliefs you hold and the feelings you experience can be so strong that you might give in to pleasing. This is a normal part of the process, and would apply to any time you attempt to change from the old ways to the new. When that happens, you can remind yourself that you will have other opportunities to practice the new desired behavior, and most importantly, remember that change is a process. I recommended that you begin the process by focusing on making small changes. For instance, you can try saying no to situations possessing a lower appraisal to you, such as situations and people who the thought of saying "no" to would elicit less anxiety in you.

Now, if you are the seriously pleasing type, you might begin by making small changes in behaviors without verbally saying "no" at first. For example, if you have habituated people to expect your immediate response to their messages, you might begin by delaying your replies. For instance, you can use "let me get back to you in a bit." Or you could reduce the frequency of times you reply to text messages, and you could reply to phone calls and e-mails after a minimum of twenty-four hours have passed. This allows for other people to develop new expectations of you in regard to your (new) "typical" reply time frame, thus re-habituating others in their expectations of you.

Once your brain is taken out of its comfort zone, it will re-adapt to match your new thinking and behaviors. Others around you are gifted with the same mechanism, and their brains have the capacity to adapt to new situations as well. So, keep in mind that others around you also have a choice to make about their own behaviors and how they choose to respond to your changes.

Therefore, your expectations of others can only be based on this very idea that "in response to my new behaviors, others will decide to do what is best for them." It is their right. "I do not know what is best for others. I am only learning what is best for me. I only know what I need and want." Others might adjust to your "no" or the new you in ways that promote a healthy new dynamic for your relationship. Some might need some time to adjust; this could be a short time, or a very long time. Others will not adjust at all.

This does not mean we will stop helping other people. It is important to distinguish the difference between appropriately helping others and engaging in care taking and unnecessary self-sacrifice for others when they can care for themselves.

Again, it is important to remember that just like you are not always aware of your behaviors, so are other people unaware of theirs. With this in mind, when others ask for favors or do not show appreciation for what you do, it does not mean they are always aware of their behaviors. For the most part, differences in how people experience things is a result of differences in perspectives, remember.

Typically, other people are not necessarily seeking your misery. In general people have good intentions toward you, and it is you who have established your roles in the dynamics of your relationship with the other person. So, if you have presented a "self" as consisting of poor boundaries or a flat-out doormat, people tend to accept and adjust to what you present. In other words, it is unlikely that others will redirect you from your pleasing, by saying, "Hey you! Stop being a doormat, and let me do for myself what I can do for myself." What you might get from the individual instead is a "Thanks!"

DEALING WITH RESISTANCE TO CHANGES

Regardless of the adjustments from others, you cannot do for them. They will return when they are ready to accept and respect you and your new limits. As for others who never adjust to the changes you make, you might need to be okay with losing them, at least for awhile. Throughout the course of our lives, we meet many people, and for a number of reasons, we do not get to keep them all in our lives. Some people move away, some get married and seclude themselves to their spouse and building a new family, some simply get too busy and are not able to keep in touch, and some are dealing with their own life challenges; this happens to all of us. The point here is that you need to be okay with losing some people, especially if keeping them will mean losing yourself. Not all relationships are meant to last. Some are meant to end, and end soon. Relationships involve a dynamic between people. Healthy relationships involve a healthy, interdependent dynamic between people. And interdependence involves two independent beings sharing a relationship dynamic that consists of reciprocity, respect, healthy boundaries, mutual regard, and compassion.

EXPECTATIONS AND THE PROCESS OF CHANGE

Guilt is part of the spectrum of human emotions. Guilt is, however, a state of negative emotion, because it does not feel good. As humans, we have the capacity to experience guilt in the early stages of child development. It is normal to experience guilty feelings for harm we might have caused others or to ourselves, such as when we violate our own boundaries. However, to chronically experience guilt is unhealthy for those involved. On the other hand, guilt indicates a person's capacity to feel remorse, which is a good thing! But chronic and consistent underlying guilt with no real supporting basis is not a good thing.

Guilt is also learned in the context of culture and family values. Some types of general values are more guilt-driven than others. Values also evolve over time and reside at both the conscious and subconscious levels, thus becoming embedded. In other words, we are not always aware of how our values impact how we think and behave. Guilty reactions are often subconscious and can be part of a person's underlying motivations and poor interpersonal boundaries, and, as we have discussed earlier, guilt appears to be a common denominator among pleasers.

Some individual parenting styles tend to be more guilt-driven, which explains where some of the inexplicable, chronic guilt comes from. Guilt-imposing parents themselves were most likely guilt imposed by their own parents, who were also guilt imposed by *their* parents…and so on. You get the point. So, should you decide to blame your parents for the guilty feelings they have imposed on you? No. Instead, you might need to begin from the root cause, if that makes sense. Instead, you can choose to move forward and redirect the meaningless and excessive feelings of guilt into feelings that are more adaptive to your life.

It is important to realize that your feelings of guilt often lack a rational basis. Feelings of guilt are learned, and they can be triggered by the response to other people's disapproval of or dissatisfaction with our behaviors. In fact, even the thought of this happening could trigger a feeling of guilt. This anticipated guilt is one of the big reasons why it is so difficult for people with poor boundaries, such as pleasers, to establish limits with others.

Therefore, guilt is a typical emotion we experience while attempting to engage in interpersonal behavior change. This is because learning new behaviors causes insecurities about how these behaviors might impact other people, and consequently how other people will view us, which becomes a worry.

We generally tend to feel responsible for another person's experiences of discomfort. We tend to take full responsibility for "making" the other feel bad. Sometimes we make poor contributions in the dynamics of a situation which is likely to negatively influence how a person will feel about us. One example of this would be picking a fight with your partner in front of your friends, instead of choosing to have a conversation with him or her in private.

On the other hand, reasonable behaviors or decisions we take, can also negatively influence the dynamics of a relationship. For example, deciding you will no longer loan your car to your neighbor because his needs to use it seem excessive and he does not take care of it. So, you decide this situation is causing you distress, and you tell your neighbor "no" more. Either way, in both scenarios you will cause discomfort to another, and as a result you might feel guilty. In the first scenario, your guilt is justified, but then you have the chance to repair the situation; you have an opportunity to act compassionately with yourself and the other person, in which case you can apologize to the person and forgive yourself. In the second scenario, you can attempt to empathize with the person and have self-compassion, since you have provided your neighbor with more than you were comfortable doing, by loaning your car to her for the past year.

In review, guilty feelings are normal and a healthy part of the spectrum of emotions. On the other hand, unfounded guilty feelings are not relationally adaptive.

ADDRESS THE SHOULDN'TS, THE COULDNT'S, AND THE FAILURES

Moving away from your comfort zone and beginning to commit to taking care of yourself, rather than taking care of others who can do for themselves, is a process that will require practice and mistakes along the way. Remember the earlier example of learning how to play the piano. You will sound mediocre in the beginning and the whole experience will feel unnatural to you. At this early stage, your motor skills are not trained with your brain to make music flow from the instrument like someone who has more experience than you do.

A similar concept applies when attempting to form new interpersonal behaviors habits. You will inevitably make mistakes because the new behavior will feel unnatural to you. Further, during the process you might find yourself insecure, lacking confidence in yourself about your choice of behaviors. At first, you might find yourself regretting saying "no" to others' requests: *Maybe I should not have done it with her or him; maybe this was not a good time for me to have said x, y, and z to that person. I will no longer be able to walk her dog. Maybe I should have waited for when she recovers from her breakup with her partner.*

Therefore, it is natural for there to be incongruity between your brain and the process of adopting new interpersonal boundaries habits, because you have not had practice thinking and behaving in the new effective way. By setting limits, saying no, and stopping controlling others' reactions, you may initially feel insecure. Playing the piano with confidence only comes with practice. Until then, you do not play with certainty.

9

Beginning The Process

Change is a process which requires that you take an active role in this entire process. This means that as a rule, you must make an effort to consistently examine how you think, feel and behave, and make incremental changes leading to a more effective version of yourself.

The very *first* step in your commitment to change is to acknowledge that your approach of relating with others has not worked for you, or your relationships. And from now on, your relationship goals will be built around a win-win approach. This means your behaviors will be framed by the win-win goal so that everyone wins. So, when you do for others, you have to win, too. This means doing for others should provide you with rewarding feelings of satisfaction. On the other hand, if the feeling you experience for helping or doing for others is one of dissatisfaction, you are losing. This means you need to readjust your behaviors to better align with your goal so that you shift from win-lose to win-win. [201]

Second, get to know yourself, and become educated about your problems. This will contribute to increasing your awareness. This can be accomplished in many ways, such as reading books like this one, journaling about your thoughts and feelings, and/or observing how you feel about specific situations. Our feelings are natural feedback about where we are, so that we can attend to our needs. In other words, our feelings are the true indicators of our state of being. Pay attention to them. You can do this by asking yourself regularly, *How do I feel today? How do I feel about this situation or this person and why? How do I feel about doing or committing to saying "yes" to this particular person or this situation? How do I feel for having not expressed my thoughts or feelings about or at a particular situation? How can I view this situation differently?* I highly recommend that you write down these questions and your answers to them. Do not attempt to do all of this work in your head. Chances are you will become overwhelmed and distracted. Writing down our thoughts help us see our own situations from a more objective perspective.

The goal is to learn all that you can about yourself and the changes you want to make, and try to observe what might have contributed and what currently contributes to your own violations of boundaries, or what motivates you to please others/ what do you fear when you say yes? The exercises in this step will increase your ability to take responsibility for the role you play in the dynamics of your relationships. This is because asking oneself questions like the ones suggested directs us to see other angles of our actions and the situation as a whole. This promotes increased awareness and an increase in your ability to see the whole picture and identify what is broken without judgment.

Third, fundamental changes do not occur as a single, one-time event. You will need to commit to having patience, as you take the baby steps toward where you want to be. It would be unreasonable to expect immediate results from your attempts to change some of your life-long relational habits. You may be thinking of Helen the accountant and master pleaser from chapter 3, who due to her health, made her life changes on a quantum leap. My suggestion for you here is to stick with the idea of a process.

Fourth, you will be required to make time each day to consistently practice the act of reading and writing your reflections. This practice will provide continuity to the process and help promote the unfolding of deeper and meaningful insights about why you do things the way you do. Decide on how much time is realistic for you to commit to your reflections on a consistent basis. It does not have to be a very long time each day (anywhere between five, fifteen, or twenty minutes all to yourself), as long as it is consistent. Besides, committing to this daily uninterrupted time for yourself should be the first step toward the positive changes you want to make for yourself. When you sit down to do these exercises you can incorporate relaxation along with it, by taking a few deep and long breaths before and during the writing and reading of your reflections.

Fifth, you will be required to get out of your comfort zone in small steps, practicing new behaviors each day, and this includes internal and relational behaviors. For instance, identify something you have been doing in your day-to day life that bothers you, and you are willing to stop doing it. Then, replace it with something you prefer doing instead. For example, you can begin with blocking "me time" as recommended in step four so you can do the journal exercises from step four. If you are married with children you can negotiate this time with your spouse so that she or he can help you have this uninterrupted time and you can then do the same for your partner.

If you are a single parent, you might pick a time when your children are sleeping, or quiet playing. You can begin teaching them about what you are doing (that is, having me time to relax and reflect) this way they will develop the positive habit of making time for themselves. You can set the timer (e.g., 20 minutes) and the children alert you when the timer goes off, and only then will you be able to attend to their needs. With some patience, your children will learn to give you that time. You can begin with timing ten minutes until the children gradually adjust to allowing you twenty minutes of uninterrupted time.

You can change how you might be attending to the needs of other people in your life in order to do something for yourself. Maybe your friends constantly call to talk about their problems, which ends up taking up all of your time after work. You might instead enroll in the acting class you wish you had time for. You will be in class when your friends typically call, expecting your attention. They will leave a message and you will call back when you can. This will make you feel better about yourself and your friends, because when we take responsibility for our own life we stop blaming and resenting others.

It can take time and patience to implement changes in our lives. Additionally, every situation is unique and some more difficult than others. However, a solution for incremental improvements can be found with determination and commitment. For instance, take a look at our next case example.

Paul

Paul is a forty-five-year-old financial banker; a father of three; and husband to Liz, who is a stay-at-home mom. Paul grew exhausted and frustrated as a result for having far exceeded violating his boundaries to accommodate for the happiness of others. It is common for pleasers to burn out after many years of living this way. To make a long story short, the way Paul was living left him with zero time for himself. Even while driving to work, his time was consumed by calls related to business and home issues. Paul reported he takes his showers with the bathroom door open, so he will hear his wife and children if they call for him. He also had a controlling and demanding boss who required a great deal from him in terms of long hours and a stressful work environment.

Paul's typical evenings consisted of arriving home late to a chaotic home life: the house a mess, the children running around, and Liz frustrated. Paul would jump right in, helping the children with homework, bathing them, and cleaning up. Exhausted, he would fall asleep while putting his children to bed. Paul reported that his fifteen-year marriage to Liz felt more like a fifty-year old marriage for both of them. The couple was no longer affectionate and had not had sex for a while. Paul did not really have friends of his own because he really did not have time for the few guys he once knew. Weekends for Paul did not deviate much from the typical week-day evenings at home with the kids. Paul was also the oldest of two other siblings, and the one his parents and siblings relied on for all different types of support.

Paul represented a chronic people pleaser because he simply did not set any limits. His anxiety levels were a clear indicator of this. He had to make a decision to take steps toward changing the way he did things. However, he felt that he could not do anything about it because he really did not have time, so I asked him these questions:

- What would you tell your children if, as adults, they were in your situation?
- How would you help them solve this problem?
- How would you convince them that it is critical for them to have healthy interpersonal boundaries?
- How would you tell them that they need to change some aspects of their life so that they can have the space they need, and how to learn how to be more effective with their lives, personally, in their marriage, and in their parenting, so that they can attain greater well-being?

Paul did not have an answer for me. However, the perspective I introduced to him did make a dent in his way of thinking, and he began to explore solutions to his situation.

POWER OF INTENTION AND CHANGE

Sixth, your intention needs to align with how you want to live. It is important for you to practice the intention associated with the aspects of yourself that you want to change. Your intentions underlie your motivations and serve as a guide to where you want it to go. You become your own intentions. This concept was well illustrated in a few studies involving driving behaviors. These studies are interesting for us because they deal with using "*intent*" to assist in changing difficult behaviors, such as in the habitual nature of driving.[13] One of these studies in particular involved an experiment to test whether a person who is conditioned to speed when driving could recondition himself or herself to not speeding as a result of implementing intentions such as "I am not going to speed." Findings provided by this, and the other previous studies, have indicated that implementation of intentions can generate reduction in speeding. Think about it! The goals you have attained in your life so far were motivated by your intentions. That is because your goals are based on your conscious decisions of intentions and actions. Therefore, the same concept can be implemented in changing your habits of saying "yes" when you mean "no." it is important to know what you want and need, so that your intentions are shaped based on the specific choice you make. It is important to note that, when you do not choose your own intentions, this also constitutes of a choice.

The study also indicated that driving habits are passed down from earlier generations. Similarly, other studies and theories have also indicated that pleasing habits, and other-focused traits (consistently placing the needs of able others before yours) are also generationally passed on [63]. This tells us that these traits are well established or ingrained in us.

However, while this is true, we have the choice of changing our behaviors by putting in the intent, and investing time, patience, and effort. Are you ready to step into a zone that's uncomfortable for you?

ADDRESSING YOUR FEAR TO BEGIN THE PROCESS

If you fear dealing with changing any aspect of yourself, you can consider doing the first and second steps from above and then the process below, because they do not require drastically getting out of your comfort zone, except for reading and reflecting (which also can be difficult, but less threatening than the other steps, because these first steps do not require putting the new behaviors into practice with other people). Once you accomplish this, you might find yourself in a better place to risk a small degree of behavior change, and you can see what happens.

When you feel skeptical about trying a new behavior (e.g., saying "no" to someone's request, expressing how you truly feel about the behavior of another person, or sharing your opinion), you can always ask yourself, *what is the worst that can happen?* Make sure you are considering a realistic worst-case scenario, versus an extreme example, that really is not likely to occur. Assess the answer to your question, such as what it is that you actually fear. Also, visualize the worst-case scenarios and what would happen if these scenarios were to happen. Then, assess whether the worst-case scenario is tolerable for you to risk by taking action. This will help you to change your perception and see things more objectively, and consequently will increase your level of comfort toward acting.

EGOCENTRISM

Egocentrism is tendency of a perceptual limitation. Jean Piaget (A Swiss clinical psychologist 1896 – 1980, known for his theory of cognitive development) referred to egocentrism as a term to describe young children's limited capacity to consider the world from the perspective of others. While this limitation is developmentally adequate in young children, this is not the case for adults.

First, to clarify the meaning of the term, egocentric means self-centered and to impose personal needs on to others without regard. However, the meaning of the term egocentric being used here was adopted from the same one formulated by Piaget. Specifically, to the topic of this book, egocentrism refers to the degree of a person's limitations in considering that the perception of others may be different than of oneself.

Assumptions we tend to make about what other people thoughts and intentions are is an example of egocentrism. This is because assumptions of what is actually happening in the mind of another person is formulated in our own heads, without having any evidence of these beliefs being true.

As we have discussed earlier, as humans we have a natural tendency to assume that others share the same level of concern for our thoughts and behaviors as we do. To best illustrate this, think of your worries as part of the context of script of a story or a film you have created in your mind. You replay this script in your mind, over and over again, and instead of the actual, real-life situation, this movie, your creation that is, becomes the source of your worries. The issue here is that you have failed to share the script of your movie with those who play parts in it (at least in your head).

Remember, you will experience feelings that match your thoughts, and if you are having bad thoughts, for example, that others are angry at you, or will reject you for saying "no" when they ask to borrow your car, then you will feel bad without any evidence of the story being true. Again, your movie and your script are only happening in your head, with you playing all of the parts. Unfortunately, these types of assumptions are another big underlying obstacle in our ability to adaptively relate with others. Egocentrism is frequently present when you violate your own boundaries.

Think of a time when you were making assumptions about what a person was thinking and feeling about you to be true, and you acted on this assumption. For instance, you reacted by doing something or not doing anything based in how you were feeling as a result of the perceived reality in your head. What was the outcome?

When this happens again take notice of what is happening. Challenge your assumptions by asking yourself what evidence you have that what you are believing to be true is indeed true. Write down your thoughts.

You might consider that there will not be another perfect time to say "no." The perfect time is when you say "*no more.*" The perfect time is now. Also, remember that often it is worse in your mind than to the person who we have said "no" to.

We do not have any evidence about what another person is actually thinking. So, when you worry about negative reactions others may have when you say no to them, ask yourself: Do I have any evidence that supports what I am worrying about?

Obstacles, difficult situations, and unexpected events will always occur in our lives. If you remember from the section on perception, we can choose to perceive any given situation in a variety of ways. It is every person's right to have individual experiences. Attempting to view a situation from the vantage point of others is invaluable to everyone. When we say no to other people it is possible, even likely to cause inconvenience or frustration to them. Obviously, it would be easier for the other person if you would say yes to their request. It's understandable when trying to see the world from their lens. Saying no to other people does not constitute the end of their world. You are not the only solution to the problems of others. You can trust that others are capable of finding solutions to their own problems.

For instance, suppose your neighbor travels a lot for work and you had been helping with house sitting. You decide to tell him that you can no longer help him. Making yourself unavailable for this task is likely to cause inconvenience for your neighbor. However, your neighbor will eventually figure out a solution for himself. *You are not the only solution to the problems of others. Through letting go, you can begin to trust that others can and will do for themselves.*

RETURN POLICY

I have developed the concept of a "return policy" to assist my clients in overcoming their boundary issues. We implement this tool at the very beginning, when clients decide they are ready to begin working on their interpersonal boundary issues.

For instance, I use this tool when a person fails to say "no" to another person or a situation, and feels stuck in the position he or she has agreed to, which often causes the individual to feel demotivated in his or her ability to self-improve. For instance, when you say "yes" and you mean "no," you can actually return your "yes" with a "no." In other words, suppose you tell your neighbor he can borrow your camping gear again, after having had an unpleasant experience with him borrowing it the first time around. You beat yourself up for being unable to say "no" to his requests, which causes you to feel disappointment and resentful of yourself, and eventually the same of your neighbor.

You decide to utilize the "return policy," so that you think about how your neighbor returned all your gear to you damaged and dirty. You also think about that you are still giving him enough time to get his own gear to borrow from someone else, since he is not due to leave until the middle of next week (and it's only Wednesday). You call him and say, "Jake, I was thinking, and I've decided I won't be loaning you my gear anymore; my decision is based on how poorly you took care of it last time. I realize it would've been best to have told you as soon as I noticed this, but I didn't, and at this point I really don't feel good about letting you borrow it again."

Usually when similar situations happen, many of us tend to be hard on ourselves for the perceived mistake we have made, especially when we begin to feel good about ourselves as a result of our attempts at self-improvement. Therefore, extending the return policy to ourselves is very useful in the process, as it helps us to self-correct in the course of the learning process, while accepting and expecting mistakes. The return-policy tool has become indispensable in the process of learning healthy interpersonal boundaries and in the taming of the octopus that resides within many pleasers.

RETURN POLICY IN ACTION

You are finally able to implement good interpersonal boundaries, and you begin freeing yourself from being a pleaser. You feel proud of yourself and start to feel comfortable in your new skin as an effective person, only to one day find yourself behaving in the old way when a request comes up and you say that "yes*ss*…" When you realize what took place, you know it is already too late: *I committed to something I did not want to or could not commit to. I said "yes" again when I really meant to say "no." I was doing so well! Why did I say "yes" to that? Why did I allow my ex to call me again for consolation?*

After this, you go back to the tyranny of should and shouldn't. You feel powerless, and your irrational thinking begins to take the best of you. You feel abused and like a victim again. You are angry. Angry at yourself, and angry at the person who requested the favor. You think, *Now I'm stuck with this situation because I already said "yes."* You feel unmotivated. You think, *I thought I had it. I'm so stupid.* For some, next comes the deprecating process of self-punishment.

Here is when *you can adopt the return-policy tool*, which will allow you to return the task to the source. You can say to the person, "I thought about it, and I realized that, unfortunately, I am not able to commit to what you asked of me, or to helping you at this time." When this happens, you must prepare yourself for the likelihood that the person will display dissatisfaction toward your actions. The person might resist in a number of ways through manipulation, such as by imposing guilt, devaluing you, by insinuating that you lack accountability and responsibility ("No, you can't do this to me. How could you?" or "I'm so disappointed in you! I thought I could count on you!").

Before you return the task, you need to prepare your mind for the possibility of a negative reaction from the other person, as well as a positive one where the person might say, "That's fine. I'm glad you told me. I don't want to contribute to the stress in your life" or "No worries. I can get someone else to do it." If the response is positive, take the time to process how it felt for you to be able to give the task back. Should the person react in a disapproving way, by then you will have prepared for that possibility as well. You will remind yourself that people can choose to have the reaction they desire.

People's reactions are based on their own point of view of the situation or the angle that shows that their needs may not be met. That person may suggest that you are uncaring in some way. Their disappointment at your declining their request can even become contemptuous. People will have unique views of the same situation, because as previously discussed, the lens of each is founded in their own perception of the situation. In other words, it is based on the person's own perception that assumptions are formulated. So, remember, just because you assumed something to be true about another person, does not make you correct.

Frequently, when your no is not well received, you might need to allow time and space for the person to deal with the situation. Indeed time can heal, because after a while the person might be able to see the problem from a less emotional and reactive perspective, when he or she is calmer, and by then his or her problems should be resolved or not. In any case, the anger may have subsided or lessened. If the person chooses to hold it against you, there is really nothing you can do. This also might communicate the possibility that this person might not be suited to be your friend, at least at the level you thought.. Remember, not all relationships are meant to last.

Try practicing the return policy when you feel that it is too late to say "no" because you have already said "yes." One thing to remember is that sometimes you might have to follow through with the task you committed to because by returning it, you are not giving the person a fair opportunity to make new arrangements. For instance, you agreed to watch your friend's children so she could go to work tomorrow. If you change your mind at the last minute, it would be unfair and would compromise your relationship with her. In this case, you might simply go along with the task and think about how you would handle future babysitting requests. This might be a good opportunity to tell your friend that you will no longer be able to babysit. This way she will have time to find an alternative to you. After all, your friend was not out to get you; she simply asked, and you said "yes"!

Again, I am not suggesting that you do not help others at all. I am suggesting for you to do so from a place of wanting, such as wanting to help, being able to help, and not always feeling obligated to help. It is never realistic for anyone to be able to say "yes" to everything. Instead, it is expected for people to say "no" to some things. You need to set your priorities straight and say "yes" to the situations that are right for you.

Think of a situation with another person who you have been struggling with asserting your needs (e.g., your partner, roommate, or boss). Examples of assertiveness include establishing healthy boundaries, of course.

- As a result of not being assertive with these people, what has the outcome been like for you and your relationships with them (e.g. do you feel frustrated, blow up with these people at times, burst out in a tantrum sometimes)?
- How is not asserting your needs and wants with these people is helping you?
- How do you think you could handle the situations instead?
- Write down your fears related to this situation, such as what stops you from behaving assertively. What do you fear?
- What do you think would be the worst thing that would happen if you were to be assertive? And how bad would this worst-case scenario really be?
- What do you think the person would think, or how would he or she react?
- Write down any evidence you have to support your assumptions, such as any proof you might have to support that what you fear will happen when you say no to someone.

- What would be the outcome of you expressing your needs, or setting your boundaries with the person in your scenario?
- Write down a positive possibility for the outcome. Write down any evidence you have that insures a positive possibility of an outcome being true. Write down what would happen if a positive outcome were true.
- Think of a time when you regretted being assertive. How would you have done things differently instead?

Repeat this exercise for every situation/relationship you feel you might be lacking to assert your needs and wants.

10

Reciprocity and Boundaries

Reciprocity is a necessary variable in all types of healthy relationships, or relationships founded in interdependence. Reciprocity also requires the presence of regard, compassion, and respect for each other, in order for adequate reciprocal practice to exist in the dynamics of a relationship. Unfortunately, reciprocity is frequently a missing variable in the relational dynamics of pleasers because reciprocity involves a two-way street; giving and receiving simultaneously, for mutual benefit. Reciprocity is a required mechanism for selflessness, which is based on a healthy motivation to give. The giving and receiving components of reciprocity are not handled by the same person. In fact, you can only be reciprocal with others if the other decides to participate. However, this is not what happens in the case of relationships involving someone with pleasing behaviors.

PLEASING AND RECIPROCITY

As pleasers, we don't behave as though we value our time and self. What we demonstrate to others is that we have endless time to give, and even if we are busy, we do not mind sacrificing for others. We can always find a way to make it happen: "*No BIGGY at all!*" Then, we begin to go crazy because the underlying script, "I'm not good enough," is getting ready to once again show light to the old belief and reinforce the script at the realization that the sacrifice will not be reciprocated.

Pleasers are motivated to give, even if they cannot give or do not want to give because of fear of disapproval by others, or because of the need to be appreciated by others. However, the pleaser can become upset when there is not an imminent return. The pleaser gives and gives, then lashes out in response to the lack of return, or stir in their own juices of a victim's grief. *How could the receiver be blamed?*

Again, the problem with that is that reciprocity is a two-person job, which requires each individual's motivation or intent to give. Pleasers often give with an underlying expectation that their giving will be appreciated. When you give to receive, you are risking being the only giver. It is important to remember that the receiver is not necessarily aware of your intentions or mental script.

As young children, we begin to practice reciprocity when we learn turn-taking ("Now it's my turn"), which is based on the concept of fairness, sharing, and selfless acts, in that it ensures that everyone involved gets to benefit. These healthy early practices of otherness also help to shape a person's capacity to relate. This concept is what also contributes to the foundation of the development of a person's interpersonal ethics.

As young children, our inability to think abstractly and, instead be more concrete thinkers, limits our ability to grasp the concept of reciprocity. For children, reciprocity must happen immediately following an act of receiving. The returned favor must be imminent. For example, a child shares his or her candies with another and expects an automatic return of a favor of equivalent worth. So, for instance, "I gave you three candies of mine, and now you have to give me three of yours, I shared my cards with you, and now you have to share yours with me, I let you play with my doll, and now I get to play with yours." This is how reciprocity works in the mind of a young child. It is about fairness. In order for the exchange to be fair, it needs to be equal and immediate (now), not later. Otherwise, it is not fair, since you got yours now.

As adults, our capacity to reciprocate or understand the concept of reciprocity develops with our ability to think abstractedly. Adults can understand the concept of reciprocity differently than children. For instance, adults can understand that the two-way street of reciprocity does not have to occur simultaneously, like the examples provided earlier of a child's understanding of the concept. On the other hand, an adult can do a favor for another when he or she wants, and without having established when and if that favor will be returned.

The development of a person's capacity to reciprocate is not only an important basic variable in relationships, but it is also an important variable in an individual's social-emotional development. Reciprocity is often misunderstood in unhealthy relationships, and this is because unhealthy relationships are made of people who are either not completely emotionally healthy or people who have not properly developed some aspects of self, or simply lack relational interpersonal skills. Therefore, some people in these types of relationship dynamics give and expect an immediate return for what they put in, while others never developed the ability to appreciate and return favors. These types of relationships tend always leave some exhausted by giving, and others accustomed to only receiving, or the receiver unclear about why his giver appears frustrated and resentful, also becomes exhausted. Quite far, I think you'll agree, from an ideal situation.

INTERDEPENDENT RELATIONSHIPS

Interdependence relates to a mutual reliance between two individuals or groups. Interdependent relationships are framed by independent parties who do for each other from a place of want and appreciation, forming a partnership between parties. They are not based on the power and control that comes from an individual's personal agenda for gains, nor do they include manipulation. For instance, pleasers have a tendency to practice codependency in their relationship dynamics instead of interdependency.

Interdependence does not involve pathological sacrifices or doing for those who can do for themselves. Interdependent relationship dynamics require the participation of individuals who are emotionally independent and regard their partners and their relationships as a complement to their lives, rather than a necessity so that they might feel whole or survive.[129]

Individuals in interdependent relationship actually do a good job of balancing their individuality and their relationship so that one does not suffer at the cost of the other. In other words, each person seeks to preserve their own autonomy within the context of a relationship, instead of fusing the individual identity with each other into one person. This is the glue that keeps these individuals happily together. On the other hand, partners in codependent relationships do not do as good of balancing their individuality with their togetherness. [60, 74, 82] This causes the loss of individual identity resulted from a fusion of two become one. This fusion leads to self-neglect and feelings of self-disconnection (i.e., "I don't know who I am anymore"), which contributes to the loss of esteem, thus low self-esteem follows pleasing.

Interdependent relationships consist of two or more individuals sharing a relational dynamic where participants perceive themselves as independent of others, but where, at the same time, the participants can rely on each other to attain a common goal. For instance, an interdependent marriage would involve two individuals who have identities independent of each other, and who are capable of relying on themselves regardless of having the partner. However, these individuals are also able to rely on each other in a number of ways. This type of cooperative does not involve "dependence" on the other. Rather, it is a dynamic of cooperation unique to the specific goals and needs of the relationship.

Interdependent relationship promotes a combination of individuality, mutuality and resilience in relational dynamics. Interdependent relationships do not exclude sacrifices and caretaking of able partners. Instead, it promotes a win-win opportunity for everyone involved because everyone is on the same page or shares common goals for the relationship. Therefore, boundaries in interdependent relationships are usually healthy because these relationships operate in partnership and the gains are mutual.

Interdependence does not necessarily mean a fifty/fifty split. The percentage is also unique to each specific individual relationship and circumstances in general, because interdependent relationships tend to address their dynamics by their distinct parts that make up the whole, such as income, household, children, romance, and life events, and so on. Regardless of what the percentage of the contribution is (e.g., thirty/seventy, forty/sixty, ten/ninety), it usually balances out because it is driven by regard for the self and the other, and it is demonstrated in all aspects of the relationship. For example, one relationship might involve the wife working outside of the home because she happens to have found a better-paying job than her husband. Then, the couple decides that the husband stays home to mind the children. The husband also takes care of the house because he is home.

This example illustrates two individuals capable of being financially independent, but in the best interests of the children (common goal), together they decide for one to stay home. This example also illustrates how, financially, the proportions of cooperation have changed to zero/one hundred without one of them becoming "dependent" because the financial disproportion was calibrated with the husband's voluntary abandonment of his career and financial independence for the benefit of the whole family. This type of interdependent dynamic can also be indicated when, for instance, a partner requires more emotional support from the other during a stressful time. Later, the same partner can be available to provide a similar level of support to his partner in the event of a life event. Reciprocity here is not inherent; instead, it is able to be delivered as needed when the opportunity arises. This is the opposite of codependency and caretaking.

INSIGHTS ABOUT YOUR OWN RELATIONSHIP

Often, the pleaser and the receiver lack insight into the nature of their relationship. Is your relationship *dependent, interdependent, or codependent?* Having insight about the dynamics of your relationships with others is also crucial in developing and fostering healthy relationships. Again, we cannot fix what we do not know is broken. So, having an objective understanding of the types of relationships you have, what your role is, and what takes place are also essential variables to develop your awareness.

Therefore, aside from the importance of becoming aware of yourself, it is also important to reflect on the types of relationships you tend to have. Reflect on the following awareness building questions: What do you seek from relationships? Do you have or do you lack self-worth? What do your relationships tend to provide you? What do they represent for you? Do you struggle to set boundaries with others, such as saying "no" when you mean "no?"

Relationship work is really work that begins with the self. Therefore, gaining insights about your self-concept and self-worth and the patterns of your behavior in the context of your relationships is a crucial component for developing healthy independence and interdependent relational dynamics.

HOLDING UNREALISTIC EXPECTATIONS

It is important to consider whether our expectations of others are reasonable, or whether we have the right expectation for the wrong persons and we keep trying to move against the current. We seem to get nowhere except exhausted and are ready to give up on ourselves. There are two general types of problems in relationships, and they are those that can be solved and those that cannot, and your expectations have to be more aligned with the solvable ones. For instance, aspects of the personality of your partner that you least like would be an example of a problem that may "not" be solvable. Unless, your partner is fully aware and wants to make specific changes in specific aspects of his or her own personality.

In other words, if you feel you are self-sacrificing for your partner and he doesn't change some of his ways which you have grown to dislike, you might want to reevaluate your expectations of your partner. First, the self-sacrifice is independently yours. We cannot hold other people responsible for sacrifices we chose to make for them. We cannot even expect recognition and appreciation for it, because other people also have free will, and, as such they can choose not to appreciate. You cannot control others, and attempting to control others is the very underlying struggle of when people engage in pleasing behaviors. Therefore, the motivation for doing for others must come from a place of wanting, because when that is the case, you don't rely on others recognition of your doing or develop unrealistic expectations that other people will change so that you can be happier.

At times, it may not be worth it to continue working on some relationships, because as previously said, some relationships are not meant to last, and sometimes keeping these relationships may be out of your control. By now, you have learned that you can only do what is within your control, such as when you can establish your own limits. However, it is not up to you how the other will choose to respond, and so after a while, you really have to decide if your expectations of the person are realistic. *If not, are you willing to continue to drain your life energy?*

We cannot continue to sacrifice ourselves for others and expect to have healthy relationships. We cannot do for others what they can do for themselves and expect a return in order to be happy. We cannot expect to have healthy relationships with others before establishing a healthy relationship with ourselves. Finally, we cannot keep on behaving in the same old ways and expect different results.

THE ROMANTIC PLEASER/THE PLEASING PARTNER

I have seen numerous examples of pleasers within the context of romantic relationships. Although the stories are different since different relationships involve different lives (each person having had their own unique experiences), the essence of the problem is often the same. In other words, there are common themes that keep on presenting themselves across different relationships involving a pleaser.

One general theme missing from these relationships is individual autonomy, which does not sustain interdependence. Instead, these relationships demonstrate levels of dependence or even co-dependence, with each one depending on the other for different and unhealthy reasons. The cycle goes more or less like this; the pleaser sacrifices his or her needs and wants for the other person. The recipient accepts the sacrifice; the giver blames the receiver for not appreciating the sacrifice and for not returning the favor, and the recipient blames the giver for being controlling. Instead of communicating what it is he or she wants from the receiver, the giver assumes that the receiver should know to read the giver's sacrifices and figure out what the giver needs from the receiver. The receiver becomes frustrated, resists the control, and says "no" to the giver. The giver gives a little more to appease the receiver. The cycle continues on, and sometimes the receiver wants to stop giving, but then the receiver controls the giver to keep on giving. Then the giver complains, then she feels guilty, which motivates her to fix it by giving some more.

These relationships lack reciprocity in the relationship dynamic where one person is sacrificing all of his or her resources (emotional, financial, time) in order to unsuccessfully make someone else happy. The pleaser in this case is often motivated by his or her need for reassurance from others. In the more extreme cases of pleasers, their actions are motivated from their lack of self-worth. They look to fulfill this void by pleasing someone else (i.e., their partner), who in turn is expected to ensure their worth. This is, again, a misconception and is most certainly likely to backfire.

The interdependence that is missing from the dynamics of these relationships causes partners to operate from within their own internal, and frequently subconscious agenda as means of survival. These relationships are anxiety-provoking because the core of their unit is founded in power and control andlacking true partnership. To sustain relationship satisfaction partners are required to maintain their individuality in the context of their relationship, thus requiring a balance between the two. Therefore, attribution in relationships influencing marital satisfaction can be linked to whether personal and marital goals are achieved or interrupted. [81]

CARETAKING AND RECIPROCITY

Caretaking is appropriate to specific situations, such as when you take care of an infant who is 100 percent dependent on you, or an ill or elderly person whose independence has been compromised. Even in these cases, reciprocity exists to varying degrees, depending on the specific situation. For example, in caring for a child, you are rewarded as you see the child developing and connecting with you, and as he or she learns to do for himself or herself, such as when he or she ties his or her own shoes. The child wants to be able to do that for himself or herself. You experience this also when the health of ill persons begin to improve and they begin to do for themselves what they can. However, doing for others what they can do for themselves and sacrificing yourself to provide a better life for another consist of an inappropriate relational dynamic. At times, it can be pathological in nature, like in the case of Leila and Alan that follows. This is because caretakers are motivated to make big babies out of the adult figures in their lives, such as their romantic partners and their adult children.

THE CASE OF LEILA

Leila, who is thirty-six, is married to Alan, who is thirty-nine.. She happens to be the classic pleaser, "highest" on the spectrum of pleasers. She grew up in an extremely dysfunctional home with emotionally immature parents, only to end up emotionally immature herself and in an abusive and dysfunctional relationship with Alan, who is also emotionally immature. Reciprocity is a missing factor in the dynamics of their relationship. Exhausted from pleasing Alan and getting abused in return, Leila came to seek my help in an attempt to save her marriage. After a while, Leila came to realize the extent of her pleasing, as it was much more serious than she had assessed previously. It turned out that she had been paying for all of her husband's expenses, including his car, phone, school, and cash deposits into his account, which covered happy hours with his friends. Alan was unable to be selfless. He did not have the capacity to give back. As Leila began to learn to set boundaries with Alan, he would at times make small returns to the favor, such as take out the trash one day. Then, he would use that as his right to an eminent return from Leila. This was one of Alan's many skillful attempts at manipulations to quiet Leila or ensure his source of goodness wouldn't stop.

In great part, Alan's expectation that Leila recognize his "good deeds" was part of his controlling traits, which at times he was consciously aware of, and at other times they came naturally and subconsciously as a representation of his programming. Alan's immature 'self' did not consist of the capacity of reciprocity or the ability to give and receive. Alan was like a child who did not learn selflessness, and anytime he felt he gave something, he needed to get his return immediately. Leila, on the other hand, who had become parentified early in her development as the one who provided emotional support to her immature primary caregivers, loved Alan the way she had learned how to love; by becoming his caretaker.

The example of Leila and Alan illustrates opposite and extreme ends of the spectrum in terms of unhealthy relational practices. The concept of reciprocity is the natural give-and-take, or exchange of support, between individuals and groups. Giving comes from a place of wanting, rather than being motivated by the possibility of a return and forming a place of sacrifice where someone is losing. When you practice reciprocity, the give-and-take happens naturally and at the right time. True reciprocity is guided by compassion, regard, respect, and love for self and others, instead of by abuse, greed, and manipulation. It is with this ability to keep this balance between self and selflessness, or individuality and togetherness, that we are able to accomplish this and have a relationship based on interdependence.

PRETENDING TO AGREE WITH THE POINT OF VIEW OF OTHERS IS ALSO A "YES" WHEN YOU MEAN "NO"

You agree with what your partner is saying, even when you don't really agree with him or her. You do this to avoid a negative reaction or a perceived disapproval from him or her. Perhaps you irrationally fear risking your partner will stop liking you, so you try to avoid making him or her feel bad or mad at you. As an underlying rule, you have learned not to share your feelings and thoughts. Instead, you comply as a way to ensure that your partner will be alright with you. Thus, you control your partner's reactions.

This way, he or her will continue to like you and admire the good person you are, which does not really work. However, you are on autopilot when it comes to your relationship. So, you do not see yourself doing things a certain way, or when you do it, it is after the fact. Eventually, you lash out! You explode and say the most horrific thing to your partner.

Your partner acts surprised: "Where did that come from? I'm shocked and disappointed in you." Then, you feel guilty.

Other times, as a result of your silence, you have displaced your relationship frustrations onto another person or situation, only to also feel guilty for acting in a terrible manner with a person who had nothing to do with your relationship problems. You think, *He's right. There must be something wrong with me.*

Sound familiar?

You are habituated to put others' needs before yours, so you do not know how to express your needs and wants effectively. You fear sharing your opinion in fear of disappointing others with your unique view of the topic or situation in discussion, or you do not have an opinion because your identity also suffered from your attempts to balance your individuality with togetherness.[74]

You have developed your ineffective habits of communication over time in order to deal with uncomfortable situations in relationships. Maybe you have learned your worth is somehow less than that of other people, and this is the frame through which you view yourself. This frame then becomes the angle from which you view others in comparison to you. In other words, in some aspects, or in many, you are comparing yourself to others whom you see as superior to yourself, or as having something special to offer you that you cannot possibly ever find again. It is this, among other reasons, that motivates you to continue with the self-sacrifices for the other person. You have most likely been repeating these behaviors and motivations in your life and you wonder why you have not had successful relationships.

It is important for you to identify your own patterns of relationships with others.

- What might be some of the common themes?
- What are some of the behaviors you tend to repeat across your romantic relationships?
- Do you find yourself refraining from sharing your position of a situation in certain types of relationships (e.g., romantic ones versus friendship) in order to preserve expectations that the other person "might" have of you?

WHEN YOU DON'T SAY ANYTHING, IT ALSO MEANS "YES"

THE CASE OF MARC AND JOE

Joe is sick and tired of having his friend Marc spend weeks at a time at his house without even asking him. The two have been friends for many years, and despite their long-term friendship, Marc always seems to frustrate Joe. However, Joe has never had the courage to tell Marc how he truly feels. Even though Joe had his own boundaries clear in his mind, he hasn't been able to communicate them to Marc. Over time, his internal frustrations have only incubated into stress, as he would stay quiet about how he felt. Joe learned that although Marc could use some help in learning to understand others' perspectives, nevertheless, it was ultimately up to Joe to communicate what was not good for him.

In other words, remaining silent about how he felt translated as a "yes" to Marc's behaviors, thus reinforcing the behavior. By exploring his own barriers in his relationship with Marc, Joe learned that expressing his feelings was not usually an option for him. He explained, "I was hoping that Marc would get the picture, instead of me having to risk telling him and have him be upset with me. After all, we are good friends."

Joe eventually risked getting out of his comfort zone, and he told Marc exactly how he felt with honesty and respect. "Marc, I know we are best friends, and this is why I believe it would be fair to you that I tell you how I feel about when you come to visit unannounced and stay indefinitely. I welcome you at my house, but it upsets me that you don't ask first and that you stay for so long. I like to have my time alone. This is why I chose not to have a roommate, which would have helped me financially, but instead I chose to spend the extra money in exchange for more privacy and quite. So, when you come over unannounced and you stay for long periods of time, you take away my privacy, and impose upon my preferred living arrangement. This is causing me to feel frustrated with you, and I don't want to feel like this toward you."

Joe was actually surprised at how well Marc took this. Marc agreed and was apologetic for causing Joe stress. He was also grateful to Joe for having finally told him how he felt. He invited Joe to adopt a new rule between the two of them, which entails being honest about how one feels about the behaviors of the other.

THE CASE OF LORI AND CHRIS

Do you often feel angry with yourself or your partner because he or she does not seem to care for your needs? You then do more for your partner with hopes that "this time around" he or she will see how good you are for him or her. The case of Lori and Chris illustrates this scenario.

Lori and Chris have been in a two-year cohabiting relationship. They have constant fights about issues they don't seem to perceive similarly. Lori buys Chris many gifts. She cooks for him, using recipes that he likes. Chris is a writer who works from home, and Lori is an accountant at a busy firm. Lori is often stressed due to her work, and she almost always brings work home. Lori takes personal days off from work to drive Chris' mother to the doctor. Lori thought she would do this so Chris' creative process wouldn't be interrupted. She also does his finances for him and takes care of his bills each month. Lori feels her accounting skills make these tasks easier for her than they are for Chris.

At times, Lori becomes frustrated with Chris because she wonders if he really appreciates what she does for him. Sometimes, such as when they make love, she feels he isn't thinking of her. Often, Lori bursts out in an angry spurt toward Chris. She accuses him of not loving her and of not showing his love for her. She reminds him of all she does for him, and that she does not get anything back. After these outbursts, the couple end up arguing, and eventually Lori begins to develop guilty feelings about her behavior toward Chris. Chris has much to learn in his role as Lori's partner. However, somehow opportunities for his development do not seem to evolve.

In reality, Chris does not reciprocate much toward Lori. The couple has habituated into this pattern, especially since Lori is so efficient with everything she does that it seems silly to bother to make a change.

This example demonstrates a lopsided-relationship dynamic between Chris and Lori. She is a pleaser to Chris. It goes without saying that Chris can improve his role in the relationship. However, Lori is ultimately responsible for her self-care. Lori lacks self-worth, and she looks to Chris as the source of her own worth. Even with the best intentions, Chris cannot provide that for Lori. It doesn't matter how much sacrifice she makes. She wants Chris to be happy and to see her as worthy, because she tries so hard for him.

So, what can we tell Lori? Lori needs to identify the patterns of her behaviors, such as what is working and what is not working. She needs to develop insight about her motivations for pleasing Chris and disregarding her own needs. She can begin by writing about these incidents and identifying common patterns. She needs to identify her own needs and express them to Chris without expectations about his ability to fulfill them.

She needs to stop her behaviors involving self-sacrifice to please Chris so that he is not unhappy with her. She needs to accept that she is not responsible for Chris' happiness. Chris is an adult, and he can do for himself. When he is unhappy, it is his own responsibility to address it. If the problem has to do with the relationship, both can express their opinions to each other. Expectations from one another should be realistic; for example, to always honor boundaries and to show mutual respect and regard. Expectations for the nature of the relationship should entail an interdependent partnership, where one person can rely on the other without requiring the other to have to sacrifice self for the good of the relationship. This involves expressing likes and dislikes to one another. If this is not the pattern, then you might want to reconsider your motivations for keeping the relationship. Again, not all relationships are meant to last.

CAN YOU RELATE TO THIS SCENARIO?

Even though you're already in debt, you use your credit card to buy a surprise vacation for both of you, in hopes that the special treat will cause your partner to respond in an appreciative manner. *This should help to improve things*, you think to yourself.

But your partner replies, "Thanks, but I wish you had checked with me first because my buddy Joel is planning our yearly camping trip with the guys for around the same time you booked this trip. I remember mentioning it to you. The problem is that it was hard enough for Joel to coordinate the trip around dates that work for all of us. I mean, can you change the dates?"

Your frustrations: You hear this and your world falls apart once more. You feel offended. How could he be so detached and unappreciative after all of the effort you put into this planning? After all, you really were not able to afford this trip, but you decided to do it anyway so your partner would feel happy. Your frustrations begin to consume you. It's simple. You are tired of trying so hard. Your disappointment consumes your mind. You then explode at your partner, calling him insensitive.

You blame him for not doing anything for you. You tell him you are always sacrificing yourself for him and the relationship, and you don't get anything back. You accuse him of prioritizing his camping trip with his buddies instead of spending time with you. Since you are frustrated, the conversation goes sour. Your partner is surprised by what you say. The conversation turns into a fight. Later, you begin to think about your partner's perspective that he expressed earlier in the argument. You begin to agree with his opinion. Next, you start to feel bad, and then guilty. Then, you become disappointed and angry with yourself. You agree that he is right, once again. You begin to obsess over the entire situation. The cycle starts over.

The reason people behave like this is because of the reasons we have been discussing all along. The pleaser here did not develop herself appropriately; therefore, she depends on her partner to compensate for what she is missing, such as internal experiences of feeling good about herself that she seeks from her partner. However, she will never be able to accomplish this goal this way. What we can tell this person is that first she needs to identify her maladaptive relationship patterns. Then, she needs to identify her maladaptive behaviors and the thought processes responsible for how she relates to her partner. Finally, she would have to get out of her comfort zone by adopting new relational behaviors that are more adaptive to healthier relationship dynamics. In other words, it is she who has to change because this is all she can do.

It is crucial that you become more selective with the favors you agree to, and be aware of your motivations for doing what you do.

REFLECTIVE JOURNAL EXERCISE 2

Think of times you felt you have sacrificed for another who did not appreciate it.

Do you believe your relationships with others tend to be reciprocal?

11

Boundaries in Friendships

"*I am always there for my friends.*" This type of expectation is a recipe for future disappointments because sometimes you might not be able to be there. Maybe you became identified as the person your friends feel a sense of entitlement toward. You are always available, and when you cannot pick up your phone, or return a friend's urgent message to talk to you about that new date, you feel bad and find yourself excusing your actions. If you tend to be a pleaser it is likely you have habituated your friends to have unrealistic expectations of you.

Of course, our friends are very important to us, but we should be important to our friends as well. It would be sensible to accept the fact that you will not be able to always be there for your friends. In other words, you can try to be there most of the time, but you cannot "be there" 100 percent of the time. Do keep in mind that you are likely one of many other friends and someone else can 'be there' too. If you happen to be the only one friend of your friend, then that cannot be your problem to fix.

It is a person's right to have as many or as little friends as he would like, including the types of friends he chooses, and all that comes with choices the person makes. Sometimes a friend does something for us and it might take some time before we can actually reciprocate the favor. Reciprocation is not the same as obligation, and as such reciprocating a favor does not need to occur imminently.

Not only can you not be there 100% percent of the time for your friends, nor can your friends be there 100 percent of the time of the time for you either. So, unrealistic expectations and disappointments go both ways.

You can be a better friend, spouse, worker, and parent when you are better able to take care of your needs. When you change your habits, and become better able to care for yourself by becoming honest with yourself and acknowledging your limitations, wants, and needs, it will be easier to be honest with others and only say "yes" when you mean it. Setting healthy boundaries is critical for your well being and the well-being of your relationships. Your friends will adjust to having new expectations of you and will come to value your honest yes's and no(s).

REFLECTIVE JOURNAL EXERCISE 1

- Think of a time when you felt pressure to commit to doing something for a friend because he or she did not have anyone else to ask. Then think about how you felt about yourself and your friend.
- Think about a time a friend who you had always been there for was not there for you when you needed him or her. Do you think his or her reasons were reasonable? Do you have all the facts as to why the person was not able to be there for you? Do you think that the same person would be there for you when another opportunity was to arise?

DISTORTED PERCEPTION IN ROMANTIC RELATIONSHIPS

Similar to all other aspects of relationships, perception is key in how we view our partner and our own relationships. When our overall perception of the world is framed by negative life experiences or dysfunctional relationships, it can influence or distort our interpretation of current relationships. These distorted perceptions keep people behaving the same way they learned to behave interpersonally in order to socially survive current relationships. Adhering to the same behaviors and continuing to practice them only reinforces them.

On the other hand, regardless of how healthy our development was, we all have had some type of experience that provided us with a degree of ineffective relational skills. Again, our relational skills evolve from early experiences in our home environment. These experiences can also be a result of "too much" love and a lack of disciplinary structure, or from relationship experiences in grade school, or from later relationship experiences when the person was already in high school or college.

Either way, less-than-good experiences with others make a dent in both our conscious and subconscious memories, and impact social brain development, and later can impact relationship experiences through our perceptions, as these past experiences contribute to molding the frame through which we perceive new experiences. Therefore, it is often the person's own frame that gets in their way of seeing what is really going on in his or her relationship.

For instance, as we have discussed, distorted self-concept and the perception of how others view us tend to influence our ability to express how we truly feel to our partner. We fear that our partner might dislike what he or she hears and eventually judge us or stop liking us. For example, I might be afraid to tell my partner I do not want to have sex tonight. I may think, *He might not think of me as sexual. He might stop liking me. He might want to leave me for someone else who will always say "yes" to having sex with him.*

Therefore, dysfunctional experiences frame distorted perceptions, which cause even more dysfunctional behaviors. Furthermore, failing to say "no" to our partner out of fear of the possibility he or she will have a negative reaction is again a form of control. In other words, when you ignore your feelings, needs, or wants and instead you say "yes" in order to ensure that your partner will remain pleased with you, this is an attempt to shape his or her reaction toward you.

Boundary problems in romantic relationships are not much different than boundary problems in other relationship dynamics, in that people struggle to set boundaries as a way of controlling the reaction of others, orin order to influence others to accept them.[120, 123, 126]

CLARIFYING ASSUMPTIONS—ALWAYS ASK!

As we have previously discussed, many of these distorted perceptions also cause us to develop assumptions and unrealistic expectations of others. We tend to assume that other people are thinking certain things of us, or that they hold a certain belief about us even though we don't know this for a fact. These assumptions do not have supporting evidence, unless the person has confessed to you that, as you suspected, he or she dislikes you, and he or she dislikes you for the very reasons you suspected.

Again, just because you think something is true does not mean you are right. The best thing to do is to ask for clarification from the person whose mind you are attempting to read. So, when you assume your partner is upset with you, ask him or her for clarification. Also, accept that he or she has the right to experience negative emotions toward you. It does not necessarily mean he or she has stopped loving you. People disagree and make mistakes, and experience negative emotions with those they love and this does not mean love stopped.

Reflection: Think about a time when you felt upset and even angry with someone you love, such as a parent or a child, and after a day or so, those feelings evaporated and you continued loving them the in the same way.

Of course, you should expect that others handle you with respect. While you cannot control that, you can always establish boundaries in order to protect yourself from being disrespected. For example, you can use "I" statements to communicate with a someone that you feel disrespected with way he is treating you (e.g., "I feel disrespected…"). As long as it is in a respectful manner, it should be acceptable for people to express how they truly feel about each other. It is appropriate to feel a range of emotions and to express the emotions you feel to the person and situation the emotion was triggered by.

It is also okay for your partner to be disappointed with you as a result of declining his or her request for sex. He or she has a right to feel disappointed. This does not mean you need to force yourself to do something against your will. We are however, talking about two separate issues here. First, you have the right to say "no," and he or she has the right to feel what he or she feels as a result of your declining of the request. On a side note, if the topic of sex is a recurring problem for the relationship, it should be addressed openly and honestly, like all other topics.

Finally, it is each person's responsibility to communicate his or her needs and wants to the other. Instead, we frequently fail to do this and expect someone else to be 100 percent emotionally attuned to our needs. Being emotionally attuned with each other, such as in the case of a romantic relationship, is impacted by our perception. It is helpful to remember that our partner's intentions are probably good, and to try to place ourselves in the shoes of the other person. You can also become more attuned to the needs of others by learning more about them (i.e., his or her likes and dislikes, what stresses him or her out, his or her insecurities).

In other words, distorted views of a situation can cause us to develop unrealistic expectations of our partner. When our perception of a situation is distorted, our partner cannot be on the same page as we are. This, causes dis-attunement. When we assume our partner should know what we need, we are placing unrealistic expectations on him or her. Your partner is not able to perceive a situation experienced by both of you, 100 percent from just your own perception. If you do not inform your partner of your wants and needs, your partner would have to try to guess what you want and need. His attempt at mind reading is likely to fail. Regardless of how emotionally attuned a couple is, it is important that each person takes responsibility to clearly communicate his needs and wants with the other.

One of the ways this can be done is by employing clarifying communication tools, such as always asking for clarification. This way you are giving the other person a chance to explain, rather than holding onto an incorrect assumption about what the other person is actually thinking. For example, you might say, "You seem upset with me. Am I correct in my assumption?"

When you play the mind reader and do not ask for the person to explain or elaborate, you will likely hold onto a wrong assumption about another person's intentions or thoughts.

Often these wrong assumptions are negative, and if you remember from earlier, our thoughts match how we feel. So, if you are holding onto negative thoughts about your partner, you are going to experience negative feelings, which will match your thoughts. Therefore, you will not feel great, nor will your partner feel great about you. This will evolve into a negative co-experience, which will obviously negatively impact your relationship. it is important to be aware of how our perception influences our experiences with others.

BREAKUPS AND BOUNDARIES

In this section, I'd like to discuss a number of topics related to ending a relationship: cutting ties, manipulation, guilty feelings, hope, and the "no-contact" rule.

First, imagine this scenario: You are a pleaser, and you finally have had the courage to break away from your unhealthy relationship. You break up with your partner, and you begin to receive long text messages from him expressing his hurt feelings. He tells you he will never forget you, and this hurts. He tells you how wonderful you are and that you deserve to find someone who will appreciate you better than him. So, you begin to engage, and before you know it, you find yourself in tears. You feel responsible for your ex's suffering, and you become his therapist. This eventually leaves you exhausted and unable to move on, but you cannot bring yourself to stop this dynamic.

Or a second possible scenario: Your ex tells you how unfair you are. How could you have left him like that? What has he done wrong? He simply cannot understand. This came from nowhere. So, then you begin to cave in, only to find yourself replying to the tyranny of emotionally disturbing text messages night and day. The conversations go from "I love you" to "I hate you"; from an attack to "I wish the best."

In the first and second scenarios: You broke up with him, and he is angry. So, he wants to take out his frustration and anger on you. People break up. It is part of life. Breaking up is a natural risk when getting into a relationship. However, it is not your job to help sooth your ex-partner through his recovery from the breakup. This is not really appropriate. For the most part, the one who breaks up has enough time to process the situation, and the other partner will be caught by surprise, whether or not there were signs.

Another possibility for the first scenario would be that he might need to show you how much pain you have caused him, perhaps hoping that you might change your mind. So, he attempts to manipulate you. If he was the manipulative taker in the relationship, he would leave this as his best for last. Again, if you comply because you "feel bad," you are basically doing the same thing, "caretaking" for an "able" person at the cost of your own wellbeing.

Depending on your ex's level of insight about how come the relationship ended, it is likely that he really did not expect the break up. How did it happen? Maybe you did not express your needs and wants effectively, or maybe you did not have established boundaries, and suddenly you burst and left. Maybe you had tried to explain to the person the best way possible, but because of his lack of insight or selfishness, you were unsuccessful in getting your message across.

A third scenario: Perhaps your partner breaks up with you, and she texts you to "make sure you're okay." The nature of the text messages then involves patronizing you; she says, for example, "You will find someone who will make your dreams come true because you are a special person. You are beautiful and smart. There is not one person out there that would not kill to have a girlfriend like you." So, she suggests you should stay friends and continues to text you as usual to keep in touch with you. She likes your pictures on Facebook, and on Mondays, she checks in on you.

In the third scenario: Often, your partner's motivation for keeping this communication going is that she wants to feel better about herself. So, her attempt at continuing to check in on you becomes therapy for her, and your willingness to engage is reassurance for her. So, she becomes the only beneficiary of this dynamic.

Regardless of how the situation was handled and the reasons behind the breakup, you need to move on. When you have strong feelings for your ex, and you engage in maintaining an ongoing contact after a breakup, you are setting yourself up for a new dynamic of further energy zapping, and more psychological damage. You would have basically changed the nature of your relationship from one that did not work for you into another type, which works even less. For self-preservation, you can adopt a *no-contact rule* for yourself. For instance, on the very first time your ex checks in on you, you can thank her for her concern with you, and ask her that it would be best for you if she were not to contact you anymore. If your ex persists you can notify them that you will block them for the time being until you have recovered from the breakup.

Breaking up hurts because it involves a loss. It also hurts because rejection is painful. Breakups activate underlying negative scripts a person has about himself or herself. Your feelings and physiology will match your thoughts. The pain you feel is physiological, and love rejection truly hurts. One reason for this is the result of a decrease in levels of endorphins and serotonin due to the stress related to the loss.

It is important to consider that once you have broken up with your partner, the process becomes an individual matter and not a dynamic of the couple. Therefore, you need to seek some type of support for yourself, and it should not come from your now ex-partner. In time, you will recover from your breakup.

Break ups can also be difficult for both partner. There are many cases where the person who initiates the breakup feels very sad about contributing to the pain the other person. So, it is not always a win-lose situation in terms of the process of recovery.

FRIENDSHIP WITH YOUR EX

It is possible to remain friends with your ex-partners. However, even with healthier relationships, it is important to give this possibility a lot of thought and time. You do not want to place yourself in another difficult situation with the same person. In the future, if you feel like having a different type of relationship with the person and it will add to your life instead of taking away from it, then, by all means, do it.

On the other hand, if this is not the case, or this is simply unnecessary, do not do it. In such a case, you can always be cordial should you see your partner around, but you do not need to be friends.

When deciding to stay friends with your ex you need to consider the possibility of he or she moving on. When this happens, your relationship with your ex will require adjustment because the new person might not be as open as you are about the idea. This often causes some degree of jealousy between the old and the new partner, with the ex in between. Being a friend is a great deal of responsibility, and there are rules to be established and respected because, after all, a friendship needs to benefit all parties involved.

Remember, not all relationships are meant to last. It is likely you have had people in your life that you did not get along with, and you will probably have more. It is important to be okay with the idea that romantic relationships involve the will of two distinct, unique beings coming from different life experiences and with their own life perspectives. Therefore, it is reasonable to expect that, at times, information will get lost in translation between two people. This could cause people to grow stronger, or grow apart.

When ending a relationship, it is also important to acknowledge that you and your partner gave it a good run, and that given the circumstances, you did the best you could during your time with each other.

Also, it is important to remember that guilty feelings experienced early in the break up phase by the break up initiator can motivate your ex-partner to "check in" on you and insist he or she wants to stay friends, which if you engage in the communication (e.g., text messages), you get to promote therapy for your ex to cope with his own guilty feelings resulted from dumping you. This would however, also promote an ongoing re-pocking of your break up wounds. Best thing to do instead, is to adopt a NO-contact rule, at least until you are fully healed from the break up. You can thank your ex-partner and let him know that there is chance you could be friends but not until sometime in the future, and stop replying if he persists.

REFLECTIVE JOURNAL EXERCISE 2

1. In what areas of your life and aspects of yourself do you believe you have the most problems with boundaries (e.g., saying "yes" when you mean "no," remaining silent instead of sharing your opinion, or asking for what you want)?

2. In which of your relationships do you believe you struggle most with boundary problems (e.g., with romantic partners, parents, or friends)?

3. What about these relationships do you think makes it harder for you to set limits?

4. What would you have liked to do differently in these relationships?

   a. Write down your fears related to this situation, such as what stops you from behaving assertively. What do you fear?

   b. What do you think would be the worst thing that could happen if you were to challenge your fear and behave assertively?

   c. Write down any evidence you have in support of your assumptions being true, such as any proof you might have to support that your fear is true. What would be the outcome of you expressing your needs, or setting your boundaries with the person in your scenario?

   d. What do you think the person in the scenario would think of you? How might he or she react?

12

When is it Okay to Give?

First, give from a place of wanting, rather than from a place of need. Give when you have the resources to give. Resources I refer to here are not limited to tangible resources, such as money or goods. I am also referring to internal resources, such as psychological resources.

Time is also a resource that is valuable for many reasons. For instance, time can be a type of financial, physical, or emotional resource. It is important to assess where your time is going. Often, we do not realize that giving our time in small to large increments can deplete one or more of our resources, whether it is money, psychological effort, or physical exertion. This can have a lasting negative effect on us. For example, you interrupt your work to respond to text messages that demand your attention, or you pick up your phone in the evenings to provide support to the same people who do not look for other sources of help because they have you. You might loan money to a friend, only to find yourself stuck later, struggling to pay your own bills because your friend was not able to keep his promise to pay you back when he said he would. Or your girlfriend demands more of your time. So, you give it to her, only to end up staying up late to meet a work deadline.

After a while, the time you are randomly giving without proper management will cause exhaustion and reduce your performance at work simply because you are physically and psychologically drained. This will interrupt your ability to be creative and/or have time to investigate your life options. Perhaps you have an idea to start your own side business or to write a book. You decide you do not have time to attain your own goals. When you stop and assess how much time and energy you actually have, and that you are simply giving to others ineffectively, you might be surprised.

For instance, often we become the enabler of friends who constantly need emotional support from us. As you take a closer look at the situation, you see this has become a habit, and the person is not really doing something to change. You find yourself repeating the same advice over and over. You have become tired because your friend who you are working so hard to help is not getting better, or, worse yet, you are not helping. When this happens, my advice is this: It sounds like you could use some feedback from a professional. Call your insurance about a referral, and let me know how it goes after the first meeting. You can develop a new habit of not returning calls immediately. Living an effective life requires using good time-management skills and being proactive.

NO ONE NEEDS TO LOSE FOR ANOTHER TO WIN
Giving is about a win-win outcome. Therefore, when you give, you do not need to lose for another to receive. Losing results

from when you feel spent from all the self-sacrifice. Giving should feel rewarding and fueling, which means it should give you energy and not make you tired. Therefore, the rule is to give from a place of wanting. This way, both the giver and the recipient always win. Another rule to remember is that you cannot fix the world. There will be many times when you cannot give, even when a situation involves others who cannot do for themselves.

BE AN ACTIVE GOOD GIVER

You can learn to create time and resources to share with others in the right context. Giving requires planning. You have to think about when and how to give, whom to give to, when an act is giving, and when it is enabling. Giving from within your means and from a place of want allows you to feel good about giving, and the recipient will feel even better about receiving. There is nothing worse than receiving from a giver who will eventually become resentful due to the giving. When giving is a win-win situation, everyone benefits, and giving becomes rewarding. You feel good because someone gets the help they needed.

Even when you have the means for giving, you need to ensure that it is coming from a place of wanting and not of controlling. For instance, you might have financial resources to give, but giving will make you feel bad or drain you emotionally. For example, having a friend who is constantly dependent on you to loan him or her money can cause psychological strain on you if you cannot say "no." In this situation, you have the financial resources to help, but you really do not want to help because you feel used.

Therefore, by not saying "no" or not continuing to give, you would feel bad, which is the opposite of good. When we say "yes," it should make us feel good, not bad. And remember that our ability to give changes over the course of our lives. Sometimes we are better able to give then at other times. For example, while writing this book, I was less available to people in my life because my resource of time was compromised. However, this will change again when I am done writing it.

OVERVIEW OF HOW OUR PLEASING SYMPTOMS EVOLVE

As we have discussed earlier, it is not possible to feel good while holding onto bad thoughts. When we feel bad about ourselves and others, our thoughts are a perfect match for how we feel. This is because we also have a physiology that matches how we think and feel. Our physiology changes in response to our internal experiences, such as how we are thinking in response to the environment. When we have good experiences with ourselves and others, we have good thoughts about ourselves, which will cause an activation of a matching physiology and the associated positive feeling.

The same thing happens when we experience bad thoughts or interactions with others. It takes place all throughout our personal development. This is also involved in how we develop our primary pattern of thoughts about the world, or our overall perception. We experience a physiology corresponding to our internal and external experiences, and over time we learn to adapt to experiencing these types of psychology. This adaptation is the inappropriate adjustment we make to deal with life, such as to feel compelled to say "yes" when we mean "no," in an attempt to not upset someone. It tends to become the foundation from how a person deals with interpersonal relationships and stressors associated with them.

Any time that there is an internal experience, there are a set of actions that take place within the brain and the body in response. There will always be a matching feeling and a matching physiological response to our experiences and thoughts. So, pleasant experience eliciting of feelings of happiness will also elicit the activation of happy neurochemicals (e.g., endorphins).

Based on this concept, at any time when past experiences are cued by a behavior within the context of our adult relationships, memories of feelings are activated. Although these memories are subconscious, they elicit a physiological response, that is a match to that memory. This will influence how the individual will react to the current situation.

Typically, when these past feelings are activated out the person' awareness the person re-experiences anxiety and feeling associated with events from his past. In other words, we will continuously transfer, to varying degrees, the way we interacted with our caregivers and others within our system, to persons who are in our lives at present.

It is important to note that any time you are in a relationship dynamic with another person, the other person also brings in his or her own relational blueprint. The relational blueprints of two different people will always complement one another in two distinct ways. One is an adaptive way. In other words, your match will have a healthy sense of self and an ability to develop and sustain healthy interpersonal relationships. If you are alike, you are likely to have a healthy and sustained relationship with each other, because you are similar in how you relate to yourselves and others.

On the other hand, if your relational script evolved from a dysfunctional system in your relationship with your caregiver, your match is likely to come from a dysfunctional environment. This combination provides an environment that can promote and sustain what is familiar (i.e., experiences of anxieties, and the need to compensate for perceived inadequacies).

Have you heard that we attract others like us? There is some degree of truth to it, but more in relation to the person's internal-relational working model [94, 96, 97]. We relate with others in ways we learned to relate with those in our immediate environment, and the same goes for those we partner with.

The way we learn to relate synchronizes with the way our partner learned to relate. For example, a pleaser typically couples with a controller. A pleaser relates by controlling the reaction of others. So, the pleaser says "yes" when he or she means "no." The controller blames the pleaser for his or her own lack of happiness. The pleaser then feels guilty and gives evenmore. This is an example of how we find a match to how we relate.

The extent to which a person's self-identity was developed determines a person's relationships with others who are the same. And for those who were poorly differentiated, [82] meaning their identity was not properly developed, they tend to find themselves in relationships with others like themselves, in order to maintain this familiar reality of relational dysfunctions.

Humans are highly adaptable and we have a brain that matches our thoughts, feelings, and behaviors. This brain is wired with the consistency of the practice of these thoughts, feelings, and behaviors. The more we practice being a certain way, the better we are at being that way. For instance, if your identity was poorly formed in development, leading to reduced capacity to foster healthy relationships, these patterns became reinforced as time went on. So, from your childhood until the present, you have had substantial time to practice these poor relational patterns. Therefore, your brain becomes a match to that.

Now, the irony is that not only are you habituated to relate in ways that are unique to you, but others are habituated to the ways you relate to them, or with them. So, when you interact, for instance, with your romantic partner, you are responsible for the role that you play. Your partner is responsible for his or her role, yet you each elicit reactions from one another and impact one another in a bidirectional manner, like a ping-pong ball bouncing back and forth. Every time the ball hits the racket, you activate the other person's feelings, thoughts, and memories.

It is important to remember that you cannot change the other person, but you can take full responsibility for yourself and for making the changes that will promote your own well-being. It is important to remember to respect others and make it your goal to be relationally ethical, which means you strive to do the best that you can to treat others around you with respect and regard, even if you are having difficulties in your relationship with that person.

Your boundaries are yours to establish and to protect. So, when you feel that (1) you are being victimized by your partner because you feel you do so much for him or her and you are not being compensated for it, (2) you are not receiving anything back, and/or (3) you are feeling that this is a sacrifice, perhaps you are giving from a place of need rather than from a place of wanting. Your sacrifice comes from an insecure self who is giving in order to control the reaction of the other person. You learned to put the yourself last, because this is how you learned.

IT DOESN'T STOP HERE; IT'S A CONTINUOUS PROCESS

If you have not yet, by now you must be telling yourself, *this is a lot of work!* The answer to your statement is *yes!* However, the work involved in changing your behavior is not that much more work compared to how much work it has been for you to deal with your ineffective relational approach.

The way you have been managing your life with poor interpersonal boundaries is in itself exhausting, and it offers no resolution. Of course, new behaviors will feel uncomfortable at first, but, again, this is true with the acquisition of any type of new knowledge or behavior. You can choose to change your perception by adopting new interpersonal habits that will improve your well-being, instead of perceiving your boundaries as rejecting other people.

The inability of James, a twenty-eight-year-old attorney, to focus on his work was causing him a great deal of distress since it would inevitably endanger his job. James was looking for ways to improve his focus. So, he would search online and through books for alternatives to ameliorate his ability to concentrate.

There are lots of programs available for this, including daily practice of meditation and organizational strategies, such as time-blocking and priority task lists. However, there will be no good strategy to improve your focus until you learn to say "no," or at least reduce to the number of yeses you commit to. When you overextend yourself, you will have trouble focusing because you have committed to bite off more than you can actually chew. Also, as we mentioned earlier, something always has to give, and it is usually what matters most to you. This process tends to begin with losing your focus, and thus also losing your ability to be productive and to live a well-balanced life.

To continue with James' case, it turned out that James had so many Facebook friends, and so many friends in general (including many potential mates) that his phone would beep constantly. He either felt curious to see who was messaging him, or he felt compelled to answer every text. He described feeling guilty for not answering the messages right away. So, again, James' issue did not involve a "focus problem." Instead, it was his constant attention to his phone that caused his inability to focus on his tasks.

To help James, we agreed to place his phone on silent and across the room from where he worked so that it was not within his immediate reach. We also scheduled increments of one-hour reminders where he would get up from his chair and check his phone. These one-hour increments were eventually and gradually increased to longer periods in between the times he would check his phone, until James was able to check his phone only every three to four hours. This change in behavior caused James' perception to change altogether, and he began to view his current behaviors of setting boundaries for himself as something good for his well-being, instead of perceiving his behaviors as "ignoring" other people and feeling uncomfortable with the idea.

When occasion permitted, James eventually even felt comfortable enough to tell his friends that he does not generally return his messages until the end of the work-day. This change improved James' life all together. He became more productive and successful at work, which lead to an increase in his self-esteem and improvements in his social relationships. As James felt better about himself, he had more energy and a more positive attitude and disposition toward his friends.

Since James was an old dog with these behaviors as he had been practicing them for a while, it was difficult at first, so he would constantly reach to where he used to keep his phone next to him. But, within a couple of weeks, he grew accustomed to the new relationship he had with his phone. Better yet, James was happier with how his focus improved, which allowed him to do better at work, and which in turn reduced his fears and anxieties. James grew more confident.

Similar to James' case, I have frequently seen situations where people have struggled with issues of poor boundaries related to their phones and emails. Anyone who becomes overwhelmed and distracted by a large quantity of work emails can use this same technique. Time can be scheduled throughout the day, such as every two hours, for checking and replying to emails.

The same idea can be implemented for returning calls. Twenty-four to forty-eight hours is a good rule of thumb for when to return phone calls. Of course, exceptions have to be made according to priority, such as when your child's day care or your boss calls, or your employees are working on an important project. In general, unless there is an emergency, calls can be returned within a reasonable time frame, and I recommend that you include your time frame for returning calls in your voicemail greeting message and stick by it.

USE JOURNALING AS A BEHAVIORAL TOOL TO REFRAME YOUR THOUGHTS

Practice makes it perfect, so staying tuned to your needs and protecting them will require saying "no" to others. This is more effectively accomplished through journaling, because it allows for you to get out of your own head. Through journaling you are given the opportunity to ask questions to yourself and provide your own answers that challenge your irrational thinking. This promotes increased objectivity in your perception of a situation. The guided reflections provide throughout the book are for you to take as much time as you need. However, for your overall continued journaling practice, ten minutes per day should provide enough time for it. Other suggestions include implementing additional practices of self-care into your life to help boost your well-being, such as daily breathing exercise and yoga. These mindfulness practices are good for self-soothing, self-care, and keeping you grounded, which goes nicely with the idea of having healthy boundaries.

Each week, pick one small aspect of your behavior you would like to change in reference to improving your boundaries. Before you attempt to change your behaviors, answer the following questions.

1. In what areas of your life and what aspects of yourself do you believe you have the most problems with boundaries (e.g., saying "yes" when you mean "no," remaining silent instead of sharing your opinion, or asking for what you want)?
2. In which of your relationships do you believe you struggle most with boundary problems (e.g., with romantic partners, parents, or friends)?
3. What about these relationships do you think makes it harder for you to set limits?
4. What would you have liked to do differently in these relationships?
   a. Write down your fears related to this situation, such as what stops you from behaving assertively. What do you fear.
   b. What do you think would be the worst thing that could happen if you were to do what you fear or be assertive?
   c. Write down any evidence you have in support of your assumptions being true, such as any proof you might have to support that your fear is true. What would be the outcome of you expressing your

needs, or setting your boundaries with the person in your scenario?

d. What do you think would be the worst thing that could happen if you were to do that, or be assertive?

e. What do you think the person would the person would think? How might he or she react?

In approximately three months, you can then reassess how you feel and where you are in your relationships in terms of boundaries. You can ask yourself the following questions:

1. How do I feel about myself compared to three months ago?
2. Did any of my relationships improve?
3. What have I done differently in these relationships?
4. What has the other person done differently as a result?
5. What have I done differently in general that might have contributed to my well being?

If you noticed small improvements, you might want to choose to continue to invest the effort for further improvement. Continue to journal your reflections regularly. Use your feelings as indicators of the types of thoughts you are having. Bad thoughts will always match bad feelings. Remember much of it is within your control to change. You can change the relationship you have with what you are thinking about, and journaling is the best way to accomplish that. This is because writing things down makes you see your situation more objectively.

It is much more difficult to work with our problems when we leave them all inside our mind.

Journal when you don't feel good and when you feel good, too. When you feel bad, ask yourself, *what am I thinking that makes me feel the way I feel?* Write down your answer, and then you challenge your thoughts by also writing it down.

You can ask yourself the following questions to challenge your irrational thoughts, which are productive of bad feelings (e.g., fear, sadness, anxiety, anger). Select a question that best fits the type of thoughts you are having.

1. What is the worst that could happen if I do or don't do what I fear?
2. Do I have any evidence that supports that what I am thinking is true?
3. Is this thought that I have an assumption, or a result of hard evidence?
4. Have I asked for clarification from the person whom I am making assumptions about?

When you feel good, you can also ask yourself what you have been thinking about that makes you feel this good. Also try to identify what type of good feeling it is (contentment, happiness, excitement), and write down your answers. Positive journals are helpful in identifying positive behavior patterns we are practicing that are outside of our awareness. Bringing to our awareness the positive things we do teaches us about the things we already do that are working. Having this knowledge facilitates future retrieval of these already existing internal tools we possess.

Here are some questions you can write in your positive journal:

1. How do I feel today?
2. What kind of day did I have today, and why?
3. When do I feel similar feelings of _____ (e.g., contentment, happiness)?
4. What have I done to feel this way? Or, what was the role that I played to feel this way?
5. What aspect of today (my behaviors, thoughts, etc.), do I need to repeat tomorrow in order to have a similar-feeling good day?

Changes involve active learning and practice. Therefore, you will not be able to improve if you remain passive in relation to the things about yourself and your life that are not working for you. Ideally, when trying to implement new behaviors or change habits, we should engage in some type of daily practice, which we have already discussed earlier. Who we are is the result of many years of practicing. If attaining improved interpersonal boundaries is your goal, that is than what you need to practice. You might begin by first assessing for areas you mostly lack these boundaries and draw up a plan that you can easily follow.

This plan needs to include some type of a daily practice. For example, since healthy interpersonal boundaries begin with oneself, every day there are many opportunities for a person to practice healthy boundaries. Your plan should address how well you take care of yourself, time for self-care, time to work toward your goals, and so forth.

First, you need to block out time for yourself. During this scheduled time, eliminate any other commitment that is not important to you. Respecting your plan is key to practicing interpersonal boundaries, because you get to say "no" whenever there is a risk that your plan might be disrupted.

For instance, let's say you want to learn to play an instrument; in order to do so, you should be practicing daily. To accomplish your goal of learning to play the guitar, you blocked out one hour to practice every night after work. However, the people in your life are not used to you being busy during that hour, and they continue to ask for things. At times, you remind them of your practice, and at times you simply fall into providing them with what they need, and postpone practice for later. Things happen; other people need you, you feel you need to help, so you never get around to your daily practice. You eventually become too busy, and your original plan fails. A year goes by, and you have not touched the guitar much at all. You feel discouraged and frustrated, once again.

When we fail to protect or take care of ourselves by placing the needs of other people before our own, we fail ourselves. We do not accomplish our goals, we take away from the things and the people who matter most to us, and we cause disruption in both our internal and external systems. Therefore, we have bad thoughts about ourselves, and we feel bad because of these; consequently, we suffer from low esteem. We often seek to increase our self-esteem, and we are constantly searching for a number of ways to accomplish this, including reading books on self-esteem, acquiring a sexy car or pretty shoes, or going to the gym. However, much of our self-esteem has to do with the extent to which we are actively *not* taking care of ourselves, which requires saying "no" to other people.

In order for you to develop healthy interpersonal boundaries, you must take opportunities like this one to practice it. This "guitar" scenario needs to be rewritten, so rewrite it for the outcome you want.

Assuming the scenario above happens to you, ask yourself again:

1. What am I thinking that makes me feel this way? (For example: I feel like a loser. I don't follow through with anything.)
2. What role have I played in not attaining this goal? (For example: I did not respect the time I scheduled to practice the guitar. Instead I made everyone else's needs more important.)
3. Do I really believe the needs of others were more important than mine? (For example: Not really. I acted out of pure habit to please.)
4. What is the worst that could have happened differently in this scenario if I had stuck with my original plan? (For example: Actually, nothing bad would have happened. For the most part, people would have been

alright with it. Except maybe for Aunt Gina, but in time she probably would have been fine. In fact, the worst happened as a result of me not sticking to my original plan of learning to play the guitar.)

Rewriting my life: I am going to learn to play the guitar. I will set aside one hour every day after work to practice. This sixty minutes is actually very little time given in exchange to someone who deserves so much more—me!

Being proactive: How would I ensure that my friends and family do not interrupt me or ask me for favors during this time?

- I will set my phone to "do not disturb" during that time.
- I will also let them know that I now take lessons every day after work, and if they ask for anything, I will remind them that I cannot, because I am in practice during that time.
- I will repeat myself until all the people around me have habituated themselves to the idea of me being in guitar practice every single day after work (the truth is that it does not take much time at all for those around us to learn).

After you have worked on your learning-the-guitar goal for a while (two to three months) you can reassess yourself. You ask yourself the same questions you asked yourself when you first failed your learning-the-guitar goal, and hopefully the results will be dramatically different from before, since you have done things differently.

Ask yourself:

1. How am I feeling? (For example, hopefully your response will be: Good, happy, proud of myself; I am now able for the first time to play the guitar a little.)

2. What role have I played in attaining this goal? (For example: I was respectful of the time I scheduled to practice the guitar. I made my needs count for sixty minutes each day, unlike before, when I made everyone else's needs more important than mine. I have said "no" to others when "no" was what I meant.)

3. What was the worst that happened as a result of me sticking with my original plan? (For example: Actually, nothing bad happened. My friends and family are actually very proud of me, and ironically, on a couple of occasions I have caught myself explaining to people how I did it. I did I develop the discipline. Also, this was an opportunity for people to demonstrate that they care for me, and have respect for me and my time. This is apparent when they say call me after practice and ask if I want to go to the movies and then ask what time my guitar practice is on weekends.)

13

Conclusion: Take Aways

- Similar to many of our habits, our pleasing traits are formed subconsciously. This is why a person is not always consciously aware of his or her poor boundaries. A person's pleasing behaviors is often outside of his or her consciousness. These traits follow automatic behaviors. In other words, just because we behave and think in a specific way does not mean we are aware of it. Having said that, again it is crucial to become aware of the role you play in the dynamics of your relationships, which means it is important to know what are your social survival skills. Both the adaptive and the maladaptive skills are skills need to be examined.. Identifying your own interpersonal makeup allows for subconscious habits to be brought to the conscious level so that you can decide if you want to replace them with more adaptive social skills.

- Regardless of how adequate our development was, we all have had experiences that have, to some degree, negatively shaped our perspective. Our perceived inadequacies could have come from too much love and a lack of disciplinary structure, or from forces outside of our parents' control, such as the death or illness of a caregiver, or from our relationship experiences at school, or from later relationship experiences.

- Either way, less-than-good experiences with others make a dent in how we relate to ourselves and other people. While we cannot change our past, we can change our current behaviors to be more consistent with the person we want to become.

- When you set healthy boundaries with others, you are really setting boundaries with yourself. We are the ones who ultimately get in our own way. We create our own obstacles. We learn to blame others for whatever is not working well in our lives. However, other people will only impact us if we allow them to. We are the ones with the guilt or the perception of feeling trapped, or who are too insecure to say "no." Other people will deal with life as they can, and your "no" is not going to be the first or last "no" that they hear. In other words, while this book is about relational boundaries, it is really about intrapersonal boundaries first, because you cannot have one without the other. Your limits with others, or the way you interact with others, are based on how you interact with yourself, the limits you have with yourself, and your self.regard. The degree to which a relationship is healthy will depend on the degree to which each person involved is independently healthy.

- There are many ways you say "yes" to others. When you don't say anything, your silence means "yes" too. It is critical for you to know your needs and wants and communicate them clearly to others. While you cannot control other people, you can choose how you want to react to them.

- Other people do not necessary have bad intentions toward you, and neither do their actions necessary take your needs into consideration. This is because a person's actions are guided by his own individual perception of a situation. It is up to you to assert your needs and communicate it to others. This can help people realize the impact their actions have on you, and often motivate them to repair the situation. This type of opportunity to ask for clarity, when you take the lead to initiate the conversation, could leave you both surprised at the realization of any misinterpretations on either side.

- Remember, it is crucial to understand that as a person, you are part of a system. Your system constitutes your internal being, how you feel about yourself, and yourself in relation to your environment (i.e., your relationships and acquaintances). When you say "yes" to something, your entire system will shift. Therefore, be selective about what you say "yes" to.

- You will always produce feelings consistent with your thoughts. When you think bad thoughts, you will produce bad feelings as a result. When we say "yes" and we mean "no," we tend to have bad thoughts and feel bad as a consequence, thus disrupting our internal system. When we experience low self-esteem, we are responding to the negative thought patterns we have about ourselves (our negative self-perception) and thoughts involving our assumptions of what other people think of us.

- Improving your self-esteem involves improving your interpersonal and intrapersonal boundaries. This can begin with minor changes in behavior. and your change in behaviors will make you feel better about yourself. It will improve your self-perception and thus increase your self-esteem.

- Becoming aware of your boundary problems is helpful, but it is not enough to win this battle. You need to get out of your comfort zone. This means you need to feel some degree of stress as you overcome your fears of saying no to others. In other words, you need to stop doing things the same way in order for you to attain different results. The process of learning for a novice is always uncomfortable. On the other hand, change is an organic process. You have been practicing your current relational habits for quite some time, right? This means that you need to be patient with yourself during your novice stages of being Mr. or Ms. Effective-Boundaries Person. As a novice, you should start small. For instance, you can employ the phrase "let me think about it," when confronted with requests you can't comfortably fulfill. Also, always ask for the clarification of others when you are unsure or insecure about feedback from other people by employing, "hat do you mean?" Again, this ensures that the other person has a chance to clarify your misassumptions of them, which frequently impacts pleasers to please.

- Often, we are writing a Hollywood plot in our heads, in which, unfortunately, we play all of the parts. The people involved simply do not have a copy of our script. Remember, we will always produce feelings that are a match to our thoughts, and then your misinterpretations of the intentions of others will cause you to feel bad in your relationships.

- Adopting "I" statements can be helpful in expressing how we feel about a situation by taking responsibility for our own feelings without placing the blame on another person, such as when we use "you" instead of "I" ("You make me feel angry" versus "I feel angry when …"). The process of learning takes time and patience. Sometimes you will do better than other times. Remember, when you go back to behaving like your usual pleasing self, you can always reasonably employ the return policy (e.g., "I did say I would help you with the project, but unfortunately I realized later that I cannot").

- Identify what areas of your life and with whom you would like to begin working to improve your boundaries skills, and start the process by taking small and consistent steps. You will notice that the battle is mostly in your head. In other words, often other people will not even feel your deeply dreaded "no." In other words, other people will do better than you think when receiving your *"no," gracefully*. After you have practiced becoming more assertive for a while, it becomes second nature to you, and others will habituate to your newfound assertiveness.

- Healthy interpersonal boundaries are a crucial component to the wellbeing of a person and to the success of all types of relationships. Having healthy boundaries is a practice, and those who practice it use it to communicate limits clearly, which begins with themselves. Healthy boundaries are the core of interdependent relationships, where two independent and autonomous individuals have partnered lives. Therefore, pleasing does not work in the context of healthy relationships or healthy people; knowing this is a good motivation to stop pleasing.

- It is important to identify the role we play in our relationships and in our overall interactions with others. While we cannot control others, we always have a choice even if the options are not ideal. We have a choice to do or not do, and to stay or to leave. Taking responsibility for our contributions and the choices we make is fundamental to our wellbeing and relational success.

- Also, as we have seen, saying "yes" and overextending yourself has a potentially greater impact today because of time constraints and an increase in imposed demands typical of the modern life. Due to this time factor and increase in pressure, people become over-loaded, overwhelmed, and stressed out. Your own life demands have increased, and so have the demands of those you please. They are too pressed for time, and you, the pleaser who cannot say "no," automatically compensates for their overload. Even though your time has not changed to accommodate your additional life demands, you take on their requests. You have less time and energy for what matters most to you. So, you are less capable of pleasing others by fulfilling their life needs before yours, and when you do this, something of great importance to you has to give.

- When our motivation for asserting our limits is ham-pered by our fear of others' disapproval, we may take any of the following actions or non-actions:

1. Not saying anything
2. Continuing to act against our will
3. Not attempting to stop others from behaving in ways which are negatively impacting us
4. Staying in situations that only take from us or cause harm to us
5. Constantly complaining to irrelevant people, rather than to the person who played a role in the situation related to what we are feeling
6. Continuing to do for others what others can do for themselves
7. Not taking charge to make the necessary changes

8. Not expressing our opinion; instead, taking the passive role in a situation or interaction, which can cause others to think we agree with them

When this happens, we can instead ask ourselves, *what is the worst that can happen? What is the worst that can happen if I disagree with this person? What is the worst that can happen if I take charge of my own life?*

- Think of a positive alternative scenario as a result of you asserting your limits or expressing your needs and wants clearly. You can then ask yourself if this is the person you want others to perceive you as, instead of who you are now. Remember Andrew from the introduction? Andrew's ability to set clear boundaries with himself and others makes it easy to get along with him and makes it desirable to be around him. Andrew's interpersonal-boundary skills provide him with an effective way of handling his own needs while regarding the needs of others, thus contributing to positive relationships with others. In other words, saying "no" when we mean it, and asserting our needs and wants, clearly could actually have the opposite effect of what we fear.

- I am not advocating a "no help rule." Humans value relationships and we feel good when we help other people. We thrive on the rewarding feelings we experience when we do things for other people. However, the motivation for saying yes needs to come from the person's internal locus of control, rather from feeling a lack of control (if I say no I will disliked, so I'll say yes).

You made it! It is my hope that this book and the guided reflections have assisted you in gaining some degree of insight into the role you play in your relationships, your motivations to behave in certain ways, why you feel the way feel, and perhaps where your behaviors came from. It is also my hope that this awareness of your own perception has added something meaningful to your life, and that it has helped promote some degree of transformation toward your improved overall well-being.

Thank you for reading my book! Now, take back your life! I'm rooting for you!

APPENDIX

Take a good look at your weekly schedule and make time each day for reading this book and reflection. Ideally, you should give yourself one hour a day. However, if your schedule is too full—perhaps you are too occupied with the needs of others—then give yourself as much time as you can. You can start with twenty to thirty minutes. Make this your time every single day of the week, marking it on your calendar for an appointment with yourself. This is non-negotiable. Do not allow anyone or anything to interfere with or interrupt your time. Set a timer on your phone and place your phone on the "do-not-disturb" mode. During this time, everything else can wait. If it is true that you want to change your habits of being a "pleaser," this is an essential step in making a commitment to self-care, rather than taking care of others. It is crucial for you to be consistent and preferably to keep a regular time for this (i.e., the same time every day). By establishing and honoring this commitment with yourself, you will begin to change your relationship with yourself by putting yourself first, at least for the daily hour (or less), for the duration of this agreement.

If you think this is too much for you, then you are not quite ready to leave your comfort zone. The other option is the one all of you already know all too well. It consists of only one step: continue doing things the way you have been doing them.

LEARNING STRATEGIES 2: *BECOME AN ACTIVE LEARNER; TIPS ON IMPROVING LEARNING*

Get yourself a notebook for notes, reflections, and other exercises you will be asked to do throughout the book. Also, do not be afraid of underlining text and taking notes in the book itself. As a general rule, our brains do not have the capacity to store all of the content on the first read. New material that is read only once, and not reinforced with note taking and revision, most likely will not be retained. The brain learns by introducing the same content over and over again and by dividing learning into organized chunks of time. Therefore, regardless of whether you will use this book or another like this one, it is a good idea to read your book over the course of a few weeks, spending a small amount of time each day reading it, completing the exercises, and reflecting on your own experiences in relation to the topic and your goals.

LEARNING STRATEGIES 3: *MORE ON LEARNING STRATEGIES*

When you stop reading a section, take a minute or two and run a mental review of the main points of what you had just read. You can review the highlighted/underlined content and notes from your reading as well, and your reflections later in the day, or at the beginning of the next reading day. This is important because reviewing the material will: (1) help ensure retention; (2) prime the brain for new and related material from the next chapter, helping you to stay focused and to better understand the concepts presented to you; (3) provide opportunities for gaining meaningful insights about yourself; (4) and, most importantly, will begin to prepare your brain to fit into the new frame you are constructing for a more effective self (interpersonal and intrapersonal) as you review the content and work on the exercises. This is part of the process of change from the current state of your brain. The learning strategies described above are suggestions that could be applied to any type of book. However, if you have a different technique for reading, retaining, and reflecting, by all means use it. This is your book and your brain, so use it in ways that work for you and will help you.

Again, this book does not guarantee your success, nor does it replace any type of professional treatment. For some, reading this book and doing the exercises may be enough to bring about some degree of awareness and change. For others, additional assistance from a therapist would be recommended, and especially in cases where a person has a history of being abused and/or neglected as a child or as an adult.

REFERENCES

AJZEN, ICEK, 2002, Perceived Behavioral Control, Self-Efficacy, Locus of Control, and the Theory of Planned Behavior. Journal of Applied Social Psychology, 32,4, pp. 665-683. Copyright by V. H. Winston & Son, Inc. [201]

Adler, R. and Towne, N. 1993. Looking out/Looking in. San Diego, CA: Harcourt Brace Jovanovich. [202]

Ainsworth, M. D., and B. A. Wittig. 1969. "Attachment and Exploratory Behavior of One-year-olds in a Strange Situation." In B. M. Ross, ed., *Determinants of infant behavior* 4, 113–36. London: Methuen. [1]

Ainsworth, M. D. S., M. C. Blehar, E. Waters, and S. Wau. 1978. *Patterns of Attachment: A Psychological Study of the Strange Situation.* Hillsdale, NJ: Erlbaum. [2]

Amato, P. R. 1996. "Explaining the Intergenerational Transmission of Divorce." *Journal of Marriage and the Family* 58 (3): 628–40. doi:10.2307/353723. [3]

Balint, M. 1959. *Thrills and Repression.* London: Hogarth Press. [6]

Baumrind, D. 1967. Child-care practices anteceding three patterns of preschool behavior. Genetic Psychology Monographs, 75,43-88. [301]

Baumrind, D. 1991. The influence of parenting style on adolescent competence and substance use. Journal of Early Adolescence, 11(1), 56-95. Bernstein, D. A. (2011). Essentials of psychology.Belmont, CA: Wadsworth. [302]

Bandura, A. 1982. "Self-efficacy Mechanism in Human Agency." *American Psychologist* 37: 122–47. [4]

Bandura, A., and N. E. Adams. 1977. "Analysis of Self-efficacy Theory of Behavioral Change." *Cognitive Therapy and Research* 1: 287–310. [5]

Bartholomew, K., and L. M. Horowitz. 1991. "Attachment Styles among Young Adults: A Test of a Four-category Model." *Journal of Personality and Social Psychology* 61: 226–43. [10]

Beaudoin, M.-N., and J. Zimmerman. 2011. "Narrative Therapy and Interpersonal Neurobiology: Revisiting Classic Practices, Developing New Emphases." *Journal of Systemic Therapies* 48 (1): 1–13. [7]

Bernardon, Stephanie, and Francesca Pernice-Duca. 2012. "Integrating Recovery and the Narrative Attachment System's Perspective to Working Through Borderline Personality Disorder." *The Family Journal* 20 (July): 239–48. [8]

Bernstein, Elizabeth. 2014. "Bonds: On Relationships: The Right Answer Is 'No'—It May Be Uncomfortable,

Especially for People Pleasers; Ways to Master the Art." *Wall Street Journal, Eastern Edition*, March 11, p. D1. [9]

Bohns, Vanessa K. 2016. "(Mis)Understanding Our Influence Over Others: A Review of the Underestimation-of-Compliance Effect." ILR School, Cornell University, *Current Directions in Psychological Science* 25 (2): 119–22. doi:10.1177/0963721415628011. [14]

Bohns, Vanessa K., and Francis J. Flynn. 2013. "Underestimating Our Influence over Others at Work." *Research in Organizational Behavior* 33: 97–112. [15]

Bohns, Vanessa K., and Francis J. Flynn. 2010. "Why Didn't You Just Ask? Underestimating the Discomfort of Help-seeking." *Journal of Experimental Social Psychology* 46: 402–9. [16]

Bordewick, M. C., and P. H. Bornstein. 1980. "Examination of Multiple Cognitive Response Dimensions among Differentially Assertive Individuals." *Behavior Therapy* 11: 440–48. [17]

Borelli, J. L., and D. H. David. 2004. "Attachment Theory and Research as Guide to Psychotherapy Practice." *Imagination, Cognition, and Personality* 23: 257–87. [11]

Bowlby, J. 1958. "The Nature of the Child's Tie to HMs mother." *International Journal of Psycho-Analysis* 39: 350–73.

Bowlby, J. 1969. *Attachment and Loss, vol. 1, Attachment.* New York: Basic Books. [19]

Bowlby, J. 1973. *Attachment and Loss Volume II: Separation: Anxiety and Anger.* New York: Basic Books, Inc. [20]

Boyce, P., J. Condón, J. P. Wilson, and B. Raphael. 2000. "Traumatic Childbirth and the Role of Debriefing." In B. Raphael and J. P. Wilson, [21]eds., *Psychological Debriefing: Theory, Practice and Evidence*, 272–80. New York: Cambridge University Press. [22]

Bretherton, I. 1992. "The Origins of Attachment Theory: John Bowlby and Mary Ainsworth." *Developmental Psychology* 28: 759–75. [12]

Bretherton, I., and E. Waters. 1985. "Attachment Theory: Retrospect and Prospect." In *Growing Points of Attachment Theory and Research. Monographs of the Society for Research in Child Development*, 3–35. [18]

Brewster, S. E., M. A. Elliott, R. McCartan, B. McGregor, B., and S. W. Kelly. 2016. "Conditional or Unconditional? The Effects of Implementation Intentions on Driver Behavior." *Journal of Experimental Psychology: Applied* 22 (1): 124–33. [[13]]

Butler, Emily A. 2015. "Interpersonal Affect Dynamics: It Takes Two (and Time) to Tango." *Department of Family*

Studies and Human Development, University of Arizona, USA Emotion Review 79 (4): 336–41. [23]

Campbell, L., J. A. Simpson, D. A. Kashy, and G. J. Fletcher. 2001. "Ideal Standards, the self, and Flexibility of Ideals in Close Relationships." *Personality and Social Psychology Bulletin* 27(4): 447–62. [24]

Carroll, Jason S., Sarah Badger, Brian J. Willoughby, Larry J. Nelson, Stephanie D., Madsen, and Carolyn McNamara Barry. 2009. "Ready or Not?: Criteria for Marriage Readiness among Emerging Adults." *Journal of Adolescent Research* 24 (May): 349–75. [28]

Cascio, Christopher N., Sara H. Konrath, and Emily B. Falk. 2014. "Narcissists' Social Pain Seen Only in the Brain." *Social Cognitive and Affective Neuroscience* 10 (3): 335–341. Accessed July 4, 2016. http://scan.oxfordjournals .org/. [27]

Chang, S. H. 2012. "A Cultural Perspective on Codependency and Its Treatment." *Asia Pacific Journal of Counselling and Psychotherapy* 3 (1): 50–60. [25]

Chung Li, Taiwan, citing C. Lam. 2005. "Chinese Construction of Adolescent Development Outcome: Themes Discerned in a Qualitative Study." *Child and Adolescent Social Work Journal* 22 (2). 111 – 128. d [26]

Cox, Sharon. 2004. "Curing Fixer-pleaser Syndrome." *Nursing* 34 (5): 64–64. Retrieved from Medical Database.

Cozolino, L. 2010. *The Neuroscience of Psychotherapy: Healing the Social Brain.* 2nd ed. New York: Norton. [29]

Cozolino, L. J. 2014. *The Neuroscience of Human Relationships: Attachment and the Developing Social Brain.* 2nd ed. New York: Norton. [30]

Cranley, M. S. 1981. "Roots of Attachment: The Relationship of Parents with Their Unborn." *Birth Defects: Original Article Series* 17 (6): 59–83. [31]

Crowell, J., and E. Waters. 2005. *Attachment Representations, Secure-Base Behavior, and the Evolution of Adult Relationships: The Stony Brook Adult Relationship Project.* [32]

Dear, G. E., C. M. Roberts, and L. Lange. 2005. "Defining Codependency: A Thematic Analysis of Published Definitions." *Advances in Psychology* 34: 189–205. [34]

Dear, G., and C. Roberts. 2002. "The Relationships between Codependency and Femininity and Masculinity." *Sex Roles* 46 (5–6). [35]

DeMaris, A., L. A. Sanchez, and K. Krivickas. 2012. "Developmental Patterns in Marital Satisfaction: Another

Look at Covenant Marriage." *Journal of Marriage and Family* 74 (5): 989–1004. [36]

Dennison, R. P., S. S. Koerner, and C. Segrin. 2014. "A Dyadic Examination of Family of Origin Influence on Newlyweds' Marital Satisfaction." *Journal of Family Psychology* 28 (3): 429–35. [37]

DeWall, C. Nathan, Carrie L. Masten, Caitlin Powell, David Combs, David R. Schurtz, and Naomi Eisenberger. 2011. "Do neural responses to rejection depend on attachment style?" An fMRI study, Published by Oxford University Press 7: 184–192. [40]

Driver, J. L., and J. M. Gottman. 2004. "Daily Marital Interactions and Positive Affect during Marital Conflict among Newlywed Couples." *Family Process* 43 (3): 301–14. [38]

Dyer, Wayne. 2012. "Are you a frustrated people pleaser?" *Administrative professional today* 1943–2194 38 (4): p. 1. [39]

Ecker, B., R. Ticic, and L. Hulley. 2012. *Unlocking the Emotional Brain: Eliminating Symptoms at Their Roots Using Memory Reconsolidation.* New York: Routledge. [41]

Eisenberger, Naomi I., Matthew D. Lieberman, and Kipling D. Williams. 2003. "Does Rejection Hurt? An fMRI Study of Social Exclusion." *Science* 302 (5643; October 10): 290–92. ProQuest. [42]

Exline, Julie. 2012. "Case Western Reserve University; Hold the Extra Burgers and Fries When People Pleasers Arrive." *Psychology and Psychiatry Journal* 1944–2718: 108. http://search.proquest.com.library.capella.edu/docview/9203947 99?accountid=27965. [43]

Feather, N. T. 1969. "Attribution of Responsibility and Valence of Success and Failure in Relation to Initial Confidence and Task Performance." *Journal of Personality and Social Psychology* 13 (2): 129–44. [44]

Feeney, J. A., R. Noller, and J. Patty. 1994. "Assessing Adult Attachment." In M. B. Sperling and W. H. Berman, eds., *Attachment in Adults: Clinical and Developmental Perspectives*, 128–52. New York: Guilford. [45]

Fifer, W. P. 2002. "The Fetus, the Newborn, and the Mother's Voice." In J. Gomes-Pedro, J. K. Nugent, J. G. Young, and T. B. Brazelton, eds., *The Infant and the Family in the Twenty-first Century*, 79–85. New York: Brunner-Routledge. [46]

Fincham, F. D., and S. R. H. Beach. 2010. "Marriage in the New Millennium: A Decade in Review." *Journal of Marriage and Family* 72: 630–49. [48]

Fischer, Judith L., Jacki Fitzpatrick, and H. Harrington Cleveland. 2007. "Linking Family Functioning to Dating Relationship Quality via Novelty-seeking and Harm-avoidance Personality Pathways." *Journal of Social and Personal Relationships* 24 (August): 575–90. [47]

Froyen, L. C., L. E. Skibbe, R. P. Bowles, A. J. Blow, and H. K. Gerde. 2013. "Marital Satisfaction, Family Emotional Expressiveness, Home Learning Environments, and Children's Emergent Literacy." *Journal of Marriage and Family* 75 (1): 42–55. [49]

Fuller, J. R. 1990. "Early Patterns of Maternal Attachment." *Health Care for Women International* 11:433–46. [50]

Gazzaniga, M., J. Eliassen, L. Nisenson, M. Wessinger, R. Fendrich, and K. Baynes. 1996. "Collaboration between the Hemispheres of a Callosotomy Patient." *Brain* 119: 1255–62. [52]

George, C., N. Kaplan, and M. Main. 1985. "The Attachment Interview for Adults" (unpublished work). Berkeley: University of California. [53]

Gilford, R., and V. Bengtson. 1979. "Measuring Marital Satisfaction in Three Generations: Positive and Negative Dimensions." *Journal of Marriage and the Family* 41: 387–98. [54]

Ginot, Efrat. 2007. "Intersubjectivity and Neuroscience: Understanding Enactments and Their Therapeutic Significance within Emerging Paradigms." *New York University Postdoctoral Program in Psychotherapy and Psychoanalysis Psychoanalytic Psychology* 24 (2): 317–33. [55]

Gottman, J. M. 1979. "Detecting cyclicity in social interaction." *Psychological Bulletin* 86 (2): 338. doi:10.1037/0033-2909.86.2.338. [57]

Gottman, J. M. 1999. *The Marriage Clinic: A Scientifically-based Marital Therapy.* New York: W. W. Norton. [58]

Gottman, J. M., and L. J. Krokoff. 1989. "Marital Interaction and Satisfaction: A Longitudinal View." *Journal of Counseling and Clinical Psychology* 57 (1): 47–52. doi:10.1037/0022-006x.57.1.47. [59]

Grabill, C. M., and K. A. Kerns. 2000. "Attachment Style and Intimacy in Friendship." *Personal Relationships* 7: 363–78. [56]

Gubbins, C. A., L. M. Perosa, and S. Bartle-Haring. 2010. "Relationships between Married Couples' Self-differentiation/individuation and Gottman's Model of Marital Interactions." *Contemporary Family Therapy: An International Journal* 32 (4): 383–95. doi:10.1007/s10591-010-9132-4. [60]

Hazan, C., and P. Shaver. 1987. "Romantic Love Conceptualized as an Attachment Process." *Journal of Personality and Social Psychology* 52: 511–24. [61]

Harvey, D. M., C. J. Curry, and J. H. Bray. 1991. "Individuation and Intimacy In

Intergenerational Relationships And Health: Patterns Across Two Generations."

Journal of Family Psychology 5 (2): 204–36. doi:10.1037/0893-3200.5.2.204. [62]

Hawkins, M. W., S. Carrère, and J. M. Gottman. 2001. "Marital Sentiment Override: Does It Influence Couples' Perceptions?" *Journal of Marriage and Family* 64(1): 193–201.doi:10.1111/j.1741-3737.2002.00193.x. [64]

Hawkins, A., and Raymond C. Hawkins. 2001. "Codependence, Contradependence, Gender-Stereotyped Traits, Personality Dimensions and Problem Drinking." *Universal Journal of Psychology* 2 (1): 5–15. http://www.hrpub.org. Modifier 2014. doi:10.13189/ujp.2014.020102. [65]

Hirsh, Jacob B., and Sonia K. Kang. 2001. "Mechanisms of Identity Conflict: Uncertainty, Anxiety, and the Behavioral Inhibition System." *Personality and Social Psychology Review* 20 (3): 223–44. doi:10.1177/1088868315589475. [67]

Hudson, W. W., and G. J. Murphy. 1980. "The Non-Linear Relationship Between Marital Satisfaction and Stages Of The Family Life Cycle: An Artifact Of Type I Errors?" *Journal of Marriage and the Family* 42: 263–67. doi:10.2307/351223. [66]

Hull, D. B., and H. E. Schroeder. 1979. "Some Interpersonal Effects Of Assertion, Nonassertion, And Aggression." *Behavior Therapy* 10: 20–28. [68]

Klaus, M. H., and J. H. Kennell. 1970. "Mothers Separated From Their Newborn Infant." *Pediatric Clinics of North America* 17 (4): 1015–37. [69]

Ito, Tiffany A., Jeff T. Larsen, Kyle N. Smith, and John T. Cacioppo. 1998. "Negative Information Weighs More Heavily on the Brain: The Negativity Bias in Evaluative Categorizations." *Journal of Personality and Social Psychology* 75 (4): 887–900. [72]

Jacobson, N. S., W. C. Follette, and D. W. McDonald. 1982. "Reactivity to Positive And Negative Behavior In Distressed And Nondistressed Married Couples." *Journal of Consulting and Clinical Psychology* 50 (5): 706–14. doi:10.1037//0022- 006x.50.5.706.

Jacobson, N. S., H. Waldron, and D. Moore. 1980. "Toward a behavioral profile of marital distress." *Journal of Consulting and Clinical Psychology* 48 (6): 696–703. doi:10.1037//0022-006x.48.6.696. [73]

Jankowski, P. J., and L. M. Hooper. 2001. "Differentiation Of Self: A Validation Study Of The Bowen Theory Construct." *Couple and Family Psychology: Research and Practice* 1 (3): 226–43. doi:10.1037/a0027469. [74]

Juvva, S., and R. Bhatti. 2001. "Epigenetic Model Of Marital Expectations." *Contemporary Family Therapy* 28 (1): 61–72. doi:10.1007/s10591006- 9695-2. [75]

Kelly, J. A., J. M. Kern, B. G. Kirkley, and J. N. Patterson. 1980. "Reactions To Assertive Versus Unassertive Behavior: Differential Effects For Males And Females And Implications For Assertiveness Training." *Behavior Therapy* 11 :670–82. [76]

Knerr, M., and S. Bartle-Haring, S. 2001. "Differentiation, Perceived Stress And Therapeutic Alliance As Key Factors In The Early Stage Of Couple Therapy." *Journal of Family Therapy* 32 (2): 94–118. doi:10.1111/j.1467-6427.2010. 00489. [77]

Knobloch, Leanne K., and Katy E. Carpenter-Theune. 2001. "Topic Avoidance in Developing Romantic Relationships: Associations with Intimacy and Relational Uncertainty." *Communication Research* 31 (April): 173–205. [71]

Kobak, R. R., and A. Sceery. 1988. "Attachment In Late Adolescence: Working Models, Affect Regulation, And Representations Of Self And Others." *Child Development* 59: 135–46. [70]

Lavigne, Genevieve L., Robert J. Vallerand, and Laurence Crevier-Braud. 2001. "The Fundamental Need to Belong: On the Distinction Between Growth and Deficit-Reduction Orientations." *Personal Social Psychology Bull* 37 (September): 1185–1201. [78]

Lakoff, G., and M. Johnson. 2001. Metaphors we live by. Chicago: University of Chicago Press. [79]

Lally, Phillappa, Cornelia H.M. VanJaarsveld, Henry W.W. Potts, and Jane Wardle. "How Are Habits Formed: Modeling Habit Formation In The Real World." *European Journal of Social Psychology*, Eur. J. Soc. Psychol. 40, 998–1009. 2010. Published online 16 Jul. 2009 (wileyonlinelibrary.com) DOI:10.1002/ejsp.674. Web.

Leckman, J. F., R. Feldman, J. E. Swain, V. Eicher, N. Thompson, and L. C. Mayes. 2001. "Primary Parental Preoccupation: Circuits, Genes, And The Crucial Role Of The Environment." *Journal of Neural Transmission* 111 (7): 753–71. [80]

Li, T., and H. H. Fung. 2001. "The Dynamic Goal Theory Of Marital Satisfaction." *Review of General Psychology* 15 (3): 246–54. doi:10.1037/a0024694. [81]

Lickerman, A. 2001. *The good guy contract: A people-pleaser stops worrying about what others think of him.* Sussex Publishers. [83]

Lim, M. G., and G. H. Jennings. 1996. "Marital Satisfaction Of Healthy Differentiated And Undifferentiated Couples." *The Family Journal* 4 (4): 308–15. doi:10.1177/1066480796044004. [82]

Maclennan, Robert. 2001. "Co-creating pivotal moments: Narrative Practice and Neuroscience." *Journal of Systemic Therapies* 34 (1): 43–60. [86]

Maccoby, E. E., & Martin, J. A. (1983). Socialization In The Context Of The Family: Parent–Child Interaction. In P. H. Mussen & E. M.

Hetherington, Handbook of child psychology: Vol. 4. Socialization, Personality, And Social Development (4th ed.). New York: Wiley. [286]

Maccoby, E.E. The Role Of Parents In The Socialization Of Children: An Historical Overview. Developmental Psychology, 28,1006-1017. 1992. [386]

Madden-Derdich, Debra A., Ana, Ullo Estrada, Kimberly A. Updegraff, and Stacie A. Leonard. 2001. "The Boundary Violations Scale: An Empirical Measure Of Intergenerational Boundary Violations." *Journal of Marital and Family Therapy* 28 (2): 241. [84]

Maguire, E. A., Woollett, K. and Spiers. H.J. 2006. London Taxi Drivers and Bus Drivers: A Structural MRI and Neuropsychological Analysis. Department of Imaging Neuroscience, Institute of Neurology, University College London, 12. 5 October. Wiley InterScience (www.interscience.wiley.com) [387]

Marchand, J. F. 2001. "Husbands' and wives' marital quality: The Role Of Adult Attachment Orientation, Depressive Symptoms, And Conflict Resolution Behaviors." *Attachment and Human Development* 6 (1): 99–112. doi:10.1080/146167 30310001659575. [87]

Martini, Tanya S., and Michael A. Busseri. "Emotion Regulation And Relationship Quality In Mother-Young Adult Child Dyads." *Journal of Social and Personal Relationships* 29 (March): 185–205. 2001. [85]

McGilchrist, I. 2001. *The Master And His Emissary: The Divided Brain And The Making Of The Western World*. New Haven, CT: Yale University Press. [94]

McLaren, Rachel M., and Keli Ryan Steuber. 2001. "Emotions, Communicative Responses, And Relational Consequences Of Boundary Turbulence." *Journal of Social and Personal Relationships* 30 (5): 606–26. [95]

McLean, Kate C., Monisha Pasupathi, and Jennifer L. Pals. 2007. "Selves Creating Stories Creating Selves: A Process

Model of Self-Development." *Personality and Social Psychology Review* 11 (August 2007): 262–78. [91]

Mercer, R. T., S. Ferketich, J. DeJoseph, K. May, and D. Sollid. 1988. "Effect Of Stress On Family Functioning During Pregnancy." *Nursing Research* 37 :268–75. [88]

Michalos, A. C. 1986. "Job Satisfaction, Marital Satisfaction, And The Quality Of Life: A Review And A Preview." In *Essays on the Quality of Life*, 123–44. doi:10. 1007/978-94-017-0389-5_6. [92]

Mikulincer, M., and P. R. Shaver. 2001. *Attachment In Adulthood: Structure, Dynamics, and Change*. New York: Guilford. [89]

Mikulincer, Mario, Victor Florian, and Gilad Hirschberger. 2001. "The Existential Function of Close Relationships: Introducing Death into the Science of Love." *Personality and Social Psychology Review* 7 (February): 20–40. [90]

Miller, R. B., S. Anderson, and D. K. Keala. 2001. "Is Bowen Theory Valid? A Review of Basic Research." *Journal of Marital and Family Therapy* 30 (4): 453–66. doi:10.1111/j.1752-0606.2004.tb01255.x. [93]

Murdock, N. L., and P. A. Gore Jr. 2001. "Stress, Coping, And Differentiation Of Self: A Test Of Bowen Theory." *Contemporary Family Therapy* 26 (3): 319–35. doi:10.1023/b:coft.0000037918.53929.18. [96]

Murray, S. L., J. G. Holmes, and D. W. Griffin. 1996. "The Benefits Of Positive Illusions: Idealization And The Construction Of Satisfaction In Close Relationships." *Journal Of Personality And Social Psychology* 70 (1): 79–98. 10.1037//0022-3514.70.1.79. [97]

Nader, K., and Einarsson, E. 2001. "Memory Reconsolidation: An Update." *Annals of the New York Academy of Sciences* 1191: 27–47. [98]

Ng, Kok-Mun, and Shannon D. Smith. 2001. "The Relationships Between Attachment Theory and Intergenerational Family Systems Theory." *The Family Journal* 14 (October 2006): 430–40. [102]

Noriega Gayol, Gloria. 2001. "Codependence: A Transgenerational Script." *Transactional Analysis Journal* 312 :22. [100]

Norona, Jerika, and Deborah P. Welsh. 2001. "Rejection Sensitivity and Relationship Satisfaction in Dating Relationships: The Mediating Role of Differentiation of Self." *Couple and Family Psychology: Research and Practice* 5 (2): 124–35. [99]

Onishi, Ayako, Yoshito Kawabata, Masayuki Kurokawa, and Toshikazu Yoshida. 2001. *School Psychology International* 33 (August): 367–90.

Panksepp, J., and Biven, L. 2001. *The Archeology Of Mind: Neuroevolutionary Origins Of Human Emotions.* New York: Norton. [105]

Papero, D. V. 1990. *Bowen family systems theory.* Upper Saddle River, NJ: Prentice Hall. [103]

Pederson, Joshua R., and Rachel M. McLaren. 2001. "Managing information following hurtful experiences: How personal network members negotiate private information." *Journal of Social and Personal Relationships* 33 (7): 1–23. doi:10.1177/0265407515612242. [106]

Peleg, O. 2001. "The Relation Between Differentiation Of Self And Marital Satisfaction: What Can Be Learned From Married People Over The Course Of Life?" *American Journal of Family Therapy* 36 (5): 388–401. doi:10.1080/01926180701804634. [104]

Preston, D. 1988. "Insolvency Specialist Doesn't See Himself As 'People Pleaser.'" *Dallas Business Journal* 12 (2): 8. [112]

Priel, B., and A. Besser. 1999. "Vulnerability To Postpartum Depressive Symptomatology: Dependency, Self-Criticism And The Moderating Role Of Antenatal Attachment." *Journal of Social and Clinical Psychology* 18 (2): 240–53. [107]

Priel, B., and A. Besser. 2000. "Adult Attachment Styles, Early Relationships, Antenatal Attachment, And Perceptions Of Infant Temperament: A Study Of First-Time Mothers." *Personal Relationships* 7 (3): 291–310. [108]

Powell, B. 1979. *Overcoming Shyness*. New York: McGraw-Hill [109]

Quinn, J.M.; Pascoe, W.A.; Wood, D.N., (2010) *Personality and Social Psychology Bulletin* Vol 36, Issue 4, pp. 499 - 511 First published date: April-02 [110]

Rankin-Esquer, L. A., C. K. Burnett, D. H. Baucom, and N. Epstein. 1997. "Autonomy And Relatedness In Marital Functioning." *Journal of Marital and Family Therapy* 23 (2): 175–90. Retrieved from PubMed.gov. PMID: 9134480. [113]

Rawn, Catherine D., and Kathleen D. Vohs. 2001. "People Use Self-Control to Risk Personal Harm: An Intra-Interpersonal Dilemma." *Personality and Social Psychology Review* 15 (August): 267–89. [114]

Rime, Bernard. 2001. "Emotion Elicits the Social Sharing of Emotion: Theory and Empirical Review." *Emotion Review* 1 (January): 60–85. [115]

Rimm, D. C. 1977. "Assertive training and the expression of anger." In R. E. Alberti, ed., *Assertiveness: Innovations,*

Applications, Issues. San Luis Obispo, CA: Impact Publishers. [111]

Rooney, D. 2001. *Legit Reviews: Walker's Message A 'Purple' People Pleaser.* New York: Penske Business Media. In D. Schnarch and S. Regas. 2001. "The Crucible Differentiation Scale: Assessing Differentiation In Human Relationships." *Journal of Marital and Family Therapy* 38 (4): 639–52. doi:10.1111/j.1752-0606.2011.00259.x. [116]

Scilligo, Pio. 2001. "Transference as a Measurable Social-Cognitive Process: An Application of Scilligo's Model of Ego States." *Transactional Analysis Journal* 196: 205. [117]

Schiller, D., J. Kanen, J. LeDoux, M.-H. Monfils, and E. Phelps. 2001. "Extinction during reconsolidation of threat memory diminishes prefrontal cortex involvement." *Proceedings of the National Academy of Sciences of the United States* 110(50): 20040–45. [118]

Schiller, D., M.-H. Monfils, C. Raio, D. Johnson, J. LeDoux, and E. Phelps. 2001. "Preventing the return of fear in humans using reconsolidation update mechanisms." *Nature* 463: 49–53. [118]

Schwartz, Jonathan P., Sally M. Hage, Imelda Bush, and Lauren Key Burns. 2006. "Unhealthy Parenting and Potential Mediators As Contributing Factors To Future Intimate

Violence: A Review of the Literature." *Trauma Violence Abuse* 7 (July 2006): 206–21. [120]

Sher, T. G., and D. H. Baucom. 1993. "Marital communication: Differences Among Maritally Distressed, Depressed, And Nondistressed-Nondepressed Couples." *Journal of Family Psychology* 7 (1): 148–53. doi:10.1037/0893-3200.7.1.148. [119]

Singelis, T. M. 1994. "The Measurement Of Independent And Interdependent Selfconstruals." *Personality and Social Psychology Bulletin* 20: 580–91. [129]

Singelis, T. M., H. C. Triandis, D. S. Bhawuk, and M. Gelfand. 1995. "Horizontal And Vertical Dimensions Of Individualism And Collectivism: A Theoretical And Measurement Refinement." *Cross-Cultural Research* 29: 240–75. [130]

Smith, N. K., , J. T. Larsen, T. L. Chartrand, J. T. Cacioppo, H. A. Katafiasz, and K. E. Moran. 2001. "Being Bad Isn't Always Good: Affective Context Moderates The Attention Bias Toward Negative Information." *Journal of Personality and Social Psychology* 90 (2): 210–20. doi:10.1037/0022-3514.90.2.210. [121]

Snir, Sharon, and Hadas Wiseman. 2001. "Attachment in Romantic Couples and Perceptions of a Joint Drawing Session." *The Family Journal* 18 (April): 116–26. [122]

Springer, C. A., T. W. Britt, and B. R. Schlenker. 1998. "Codependency: Clarifying The Construct." *Journal of Mental Health Counseling* 20: 141–58. [127]

Sroufe, L. A., and E. Waters. 1977. "Attachment As An Organizational Construct." *Child Development* 48: 1184–99. [131]

Stafford, L. L. 2001. "Is Codependency A Meaningful Concept?" *Issues in Mental Health Nursing* 22: 273–86. [128]

Starner, R. 2001. *People pleasers.* Conway Data. [123]

Steiner, Marianne, Mathias Allemand, and Michael E. McCullough. "Do Agreeableness and Neuroticism Explain Age Differences in the Tendency to Forgive Others? *Personal Sociology, Psychological Bulletin* 38 (April 2012): 441–53. [124]

Steele, Curtis. 2001. "The Neuroscience of Psychotherapy: Healing the Social Brain." *Transactional Analysis Journal* 42 (2): Psychology Database pg. 155. [132]

Story, L. B., B. R. Karney, E. Lawrence, and T. N. Bradbury. 2001. "Interpersonal Mediators In The Intergenerational Transmission Of Marital Dysfunction." *Journal of Family Psychology* 18 (3): 519–29. doi:10.1037/0893-3200.18.3.519. [125]

Svoboda, E. 2001. *May I Serve As Your Doormat? Why Are Some People So Focused On Pleasing Others That They Sacrifice Their Own Needs? (Field Guide to the People-Pleaser)*. Sussex Publishers. [126]

Roberts, J. E., I. H. Gotlib, And J. D. Kassel. 1996. "Adult Attachment Security And Symptoms Of Depression: The Mediating Roles Of Dysfunctional Attitudes And Low Self-Esteem." *Journal of Personality and Social Psychology* 70: 310–20. [133]

Toomey, B., and B. Ecker. 2001. "Of Neurons And Knowings: Constructivism, Coherence Psychology, And Their Neurodynamic Substrates." *Journal Of Constructivist Psychology* 20: 201–45. [134]

Weldon, D. 2001. *In This Economy, "People Pleasers" Can Be Workers' Best Friends*. Chicago: MediaTec Publishing. [135]

Wells, M. C., M. B. Hill, G. Brack, C. J. Brack, and E. E. Firestone. 2001. "Codependency's Relationships To Defining Characteristics In College Students." *Journal of College Student Psychotherapy* 20 (4): 71–84. doi:10.1300/J035v20n04_07. [139]

Wells, M., C. Glickauf-Hughes, and R. Jones. 1999. "Codependency: A Grass Roots Construct's Relationship To Shame-Proneness, Low Self-Esteem, And Childhood

Parentification." *American Journal of Family Therapy* 27: 63–71. [138]

Zakowski, S. G., C. G. McAllister, M. Deal, and A. Baum. 1992. "Stress, Reactivity, And Immune Function In Healthy Men." *Health Psychology* 11 (4): 223–32. doi:10.1037/0278-6133.11.4.223. [136]

Zvelc, Gregor. 1998. "Relational Schemas Theory and Transactional Analysis." *Transactional Analysis Journal* 28 (January): 83–87. [137]